THIS JOURNAL BELONGS TO:

........................................................

# ALL THINGS ARE POSSIBLE

## A GUIDED JOURNAL FOR CHRISTIAN WOMEN WITH INSPIRING BIBLE VERSES AND CREATIVE PROMPTS

MELANIE REDD

Illustrations by Enya Todd

ROCKRIDGE PRESS

Interior and Cover Designer: Tricia Jang
Art Producer: Samantha Ulban
Editor: Meera Pal
Production Editor: Ruth Sakata Corley

Illustrations © 2020 Enya Todd. Author Photo Courtesy of Randy Redd

ISBN: 978-1-64739-953-5

R0

This journal is dedicated to every woman who wants to experience a sweeter relationship with the Lord Jesus. I pray that as you read these scriptures, consider these reflections, and journal your thoughts, you will draw a little closer to the Lord.

# INTRODUCTION

It all began with a wide-ruled spiral notebook and a number two pencil.

Since I was a little girl, I have loved to write. From diaries and journals to short stories in elementary school, I've been making notes and putting words on paper for a long time.

When I was a new Christ-follower in middle school, one of my mentors gave me a devotional notebook that I used to journal as I read, studied, and prayed. Writing and journaling have helped take my relationship with the Lord to higher heights and greater depths. I've drawn closer to Jesus as I've journaled.

To this day, I keep a devotional notebook by my side as I pray and read the Bible. When something encourages me, I write it down. As I come across a great verse or quote, I jot that down, as well. Taking notes has enabled me to stay focused, remember what I am reading, and look back at how I have grown up in the Lord. Indeed, writing can be a powerful tool for any woman who would like to grow closer to the Lord.

There is something about reading scripture, thinking about what you are read-ing, and then applying it to your own circumstances that is life changing. To actually pen these ideas onto paper helps bind them to your heart and life.

That is what this journal is all about. It's your opportunity to spend a few moments basking in scripture's truth, considering how it impacts you personally, and then taking the time to express your thoughts on paper.

The verses and reflections have been carefully and prayerfully chosen just for you with a focus on 10 specific areas of spiritual growth. These areas were chosen to inspire your devotional journey and to challenge and affirm you.

It is my hope and prayer that you will be encouraged to study a little more, think a little more, reflect a little more, and pray a little more. May you take time each day to consider and write about what you are learning. May God propel you forward in your relationship with Him and with others.

I am praying that you will be blessed as you read, study, contemplate, pray, and journal. May the days ahead be some of the most amazing days you've ever experienced.

The words of Numbers 6:24–26, New King James Version, form my prayer for you:

The Lord bless you and keep you;
The Lord make His face shine upon you,
And be gracious to you;
The Lord lift up His countenance upon you,
And give you peace.

Blessings to you,
Melanie Redd

# HOW TO USE THIS JOURNAL

Welcome to your journal!

The Bible is a powerful book, and I believe that you will experience much hope, victory, and joy as you spend devotional time with the Lord each day through this journal.

For the Christian woman who wants to grow closer to the Lord, I hope this journal will be an inspiring resource that you can incorporate into your daily life. It includes 90 meaningful and thought-provoking Bible verses intended to guide you on your path of spiritual growth. Each verse has been carefully chosen to offer you wisdom, direction, and encouragement. The verses come from the King James Version (KJV), the New King James Version (NKJV), the New International Version (NIV), and The Message (MSG).

Accompanying each verse, you will find a prompt for reflection to guide you as you pray, consider, and apply the scripture you have read for that particular day. Take a few minutes to interact with the truths, and then write down your thoughts, ideas, and prayers. These steps can be life altering!

The chosen verses each speak to one of these 10 areas of your life: joy, peace, patience, kindness, faithfulness, self-discipline, gratitude, acts of service, forgiveness, and love.

Today is a great day to begin. So, turn the page, grab your favorite pen or pencil, and get started!

Then he said unto them,
Go your way, eat the fat, and drink the
sweet, and send portions unto them for
whom nothing is prepared: for this day
is holy unto our Lord: neither be ye sorry;
for the joy of the Lord is your strength.

*Nehemiah 8:10, KJV*

This passage is about God's wish for us to celebrate and rejoice on holy days. What brings you joy
on holy days? What might you want to incorporate
more of into your worship?

Blessed are the
peacemakers: for they
shall be called the
children of God.

*Matthew 5:9, KJV*

From this scripture verse, we learn that God loves
peacemakers. Take a minute to think about the
peacemakers you know. In the space provided,
describe what you have seen them do to sow peace.

Rejoicing in hope;
patient in tribulation;
continuing instant
in prayer.

*Romans 12:12, KJV*

Life is more a marathon than a sprint. Many days
are full of the mundane and the necessary. If a
close friend were to tell you she was discouraged,
how might you help her wait with more patience?

When she speaks
she has something
worthwhile to say, and she
always says it kindly.

*Proverbs 31:26, MSG*

Are you a woman who speaks with wisdom and
kindness? If you were to ask those closest to you
to assess your speech, what might they say? Finish
this thought: My friends and family would say that
when I speak, I speak with . . .

But Ruth replied, "Don't urge me to leave you or to turn back from you. Where you go I will go, and where you stay I will stay. Your people will be my people and your God my God."

*Ruth 1:16, NIV*

These words were spoken by a daughter-in-law to her mother-in-law, whom she dearly loves, promising to be loyal and faithful to her. Think about the women in your life. Write down the names of two or three women who have been exceedingly loyal and faithful to you. Why do you appreciate them? Take a little time to thank each one today.

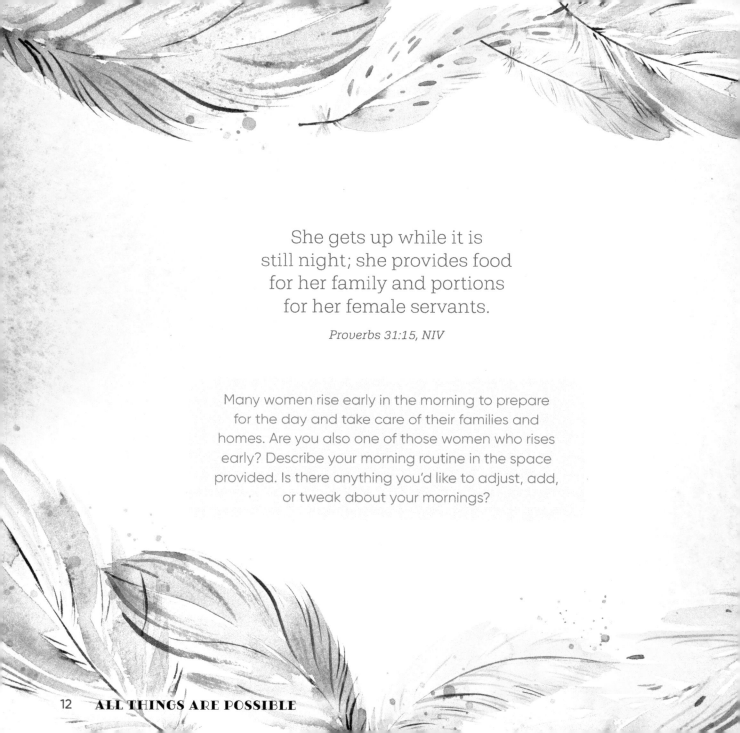

She gets up while it is
still night; she provides food
for her family and portions
for her female servants.

*Proverbs 31:15, NIV*

Many women rise early in the morning to prepare
for the day and take care of their families and
homes. Are you also one of those women who rises
early? Describe your morning routine in the space
provided. Is there anything you'd like to adjust, add,
or tweak about your mornings?

Give her of the fruit
of her hands; and let her
own works praise her
in the gates.

*Proverbs 31:31, KJV*

If your friends, family, and co-workers praised you
today, what sorts of things would you hope they
would say? What do you want to be known and
thanked for?

One of those listening was a woman from the city of Thyatira named Lydia, a dealer in purple cloth. She was a worshiper of God. The Lord opened her heart to respond to Paul's message. When she and the members of her household were baptized, she invited us to her home. "If you consider me a believer in the Lord," she said, "come and stay at my house." And she persuaded us.

*Acts 16:14–15, NIV*

Lydia is remembered for her hospitality. What about you? Are you a hospitable woman? List three to four ways that you are currently showing hospitality to others—neighbors, co-workers, friends, and family members.

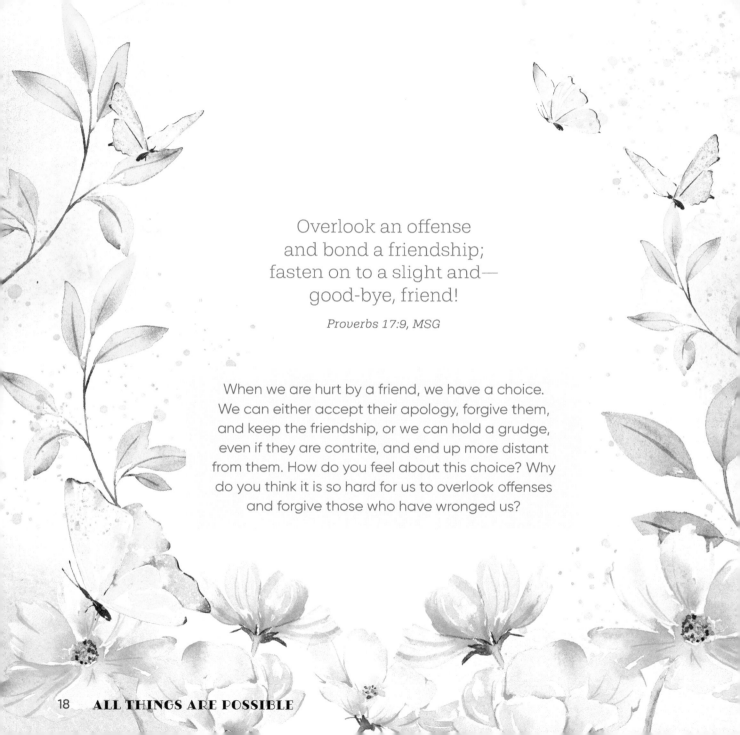

Overlook an offense
and bond a friendship;
fasten on to a slight and—
good-bye, friend!

*Proverbs 17:9, MSG*

When we are hurt by a friend, we have a choice.
We can either accept their apology, forgive them,
and keep the friendship, or we can hold a grudge,
even if they are contrite, and end up more distant
from them. How do you feel about this choice? Why
do you think it is so hard for us to overlook offenses
and forgive those who have wronged us?

For I am convinced that neither death nor life, neither angels nor demons, neither the present nor the future, nor any powers, neither height nor depth, nor anything else in all creation, will be able to separate us from the love of God that is in Christ Jesus our Lord.

*Romans 8:38–39, NIV*

If you've ever been separated from your friends or family members for an extended period of time, you know how hard it can be. We are people who like to stay connected to others. From this scripture passage, we learn that absolutely nothing can separate us from God's love for us. How does knowing this make you feel?

If ye keep my commandments, ye shall abide in my love; even as I have kept my Father's commandments and abide in his love. These things have I spoken unto you, that my joy might remain in you, and that your joy might be full.

*John 15:10–11, KJV*

What wonderful words from the Lord Jesus! He promised that our joy would remain and be full as we follow Him, keep His commandments, and stay close to Him. Think about your relationship with the Lord. In what ways has keeping Jesus's commandments added joy to your life?

Great peace have they
which love thy law: and
nothing shall offend them.

*Psalm 119:165, KJV*

What is your relationship to the Bible? Do you
love it or want to love it? Read today's verse
once more and complete this sentence:
I think if I were to love the Bible more,
my life might change in these ways . . .

The Lord shall fight
for you, and ye shall
hold your peace.

*Exodus 14:14, KJV*

Waiting on God can be a challenge. To hold our peace, to be still, and to trust Him can be one of the hardest things in the Christian life. It can be close to impossible. Knowing He promises to fight for you, what are some practical ways you have found to wait on Him?

And be kind to one another, tenderhearted, forgiving one another, even as God in Christ forgave you.

*Ephesians 4:32, NKJV*

Author Bob Goff is credited with saying, "Throw kindness around like confetti." How might we impact the lives of our family members, neighbors, co-workers, and friends if we were to become astonishingly kind? Write down two to three kind acts you've done in the past week. What more can you do to "throw kindness around like confetti"?

"His master replied, 'Well done, good and faithful servant! You have been faithful with a few things; I will put you in charge of many things. Come and share your master's happiness!'"

*Matthew 25:21, NIV*

Faithfulness in handling the small things (the dishes, laundry, cooking) is not the most glamourous life endeavor. And yet, Jesus applauded it, pledging more to those who were faithful with little. Make a list of 10 small ways that you faithfully fulfill your obligations. Then, pray over that list and invite God to give you more and bigger things to do.

Likewise, teach the older women to be reverent in the way they live, not to be slanderers or addicted to much wine, but to teach what is good.

*Titus 2:3, NIV*

In this particular passage, the older women are encouraged to model and instruct the younger women to be wise in the way they live, in the way they speak, and in the way they drink. Looking at your own life, are there any areas in which you'd like to be wiser?

Pray diligently.
Stay alert, with
your eyes wide
open in gratitude.

*Colossians 4:2, MSG*

It is easy to turn our prayers into a list of petitions: asking for things, seeking answers, and lifting up needs. However, the Bible reminds us to pray with gratitude. What if you added more gratitude to your prayers? Write down 15 things you are thankful for, then take a moment to thank God for each one.

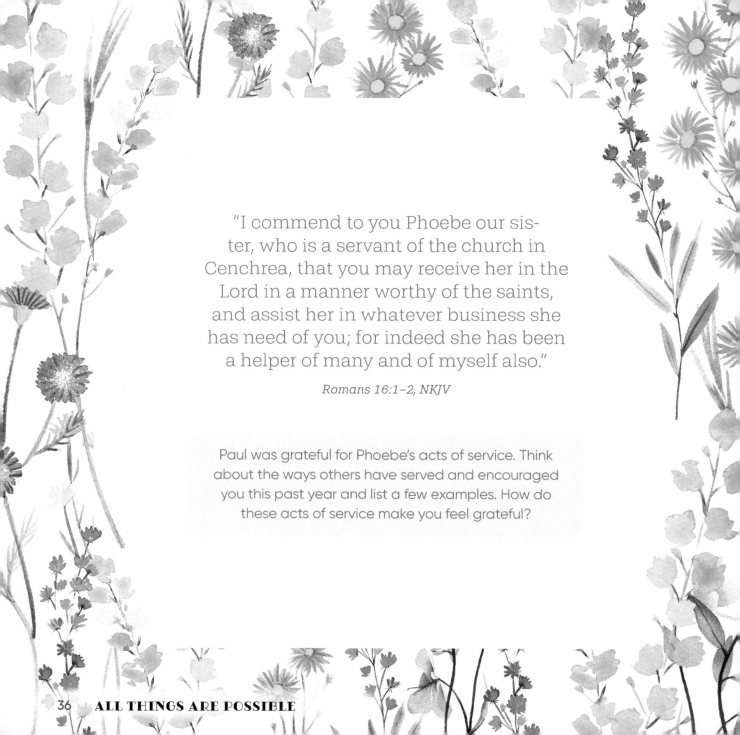

"I commend to you Phoebe our sister, who is a servant of the church in Cenchrea, that you may receive her in the Lord in a manner worthy of the saints, and assist her in whatever business she has need of you; for indeed she has been a helper of many and of myself also."

*Romans 16:1–2, NKJV*

Paul was grateful for Phoebe's acts of service. Think about the ways others have served and encouraged you this past year and list a few examples. How do these acts of service make you feel grateful?

When Jesus had raised Himself up and saw no one but the woman, He said to her, "Woman, where are those accusers of yours? Has no one condemned you?" She said, "No one, Lord." And Jesus said to her, "Neither do I condemn you; go and sin no more."

*John 8:10–11, NKJV*

Forgiveness is a rare and a special gift. It's a choice we all get to make, especially in the face of hurt or betrayal. Is there someone you need to give the gift of grace to right now? Pray about the situation and write your thoughts.

Love is patient, love is kind. It does not envy, it does not boast, it is not proud. It does not dishonor others, it is not self-seeking, it is not easily angered, it keeps no record of wrongs.

*1 Corinthians 13:4–5, NIV*

Defining love is a challenge, but the Bible gives us a list of traits that exemplify love. Read over the descriptions in the verses above. Which of these traits do you find most difficult to exemplify in your closest relationships? Which do you find to be the easiest to enact?

My brethren, count it all
joy when ye fall into divers
temptations; knowing this,
that the trying of your faith
worketh patience.

*James 1:2–3, KJV*

Pause and think about a recent temptation, test,
or trial. Maybe it was a loss, an illness, or a huge
life change. Consider some ways you can rejoice
because of how you grew and learned through this
trial. Write about the joy that ultimately came out
of this difficult season.

Peace I leave with you, my peace I give unto you: not as the world giveth, give I unto you. Let not your heart be troubled, neither let it be afraid.

*John 14:27, KJV*

Jesus promised His followers that they would experience peace over trouble, fear, and this world. What does Christ's peace look like? Reflect on a time when you personally experienced God's peace.

With all lowliness and meekness,
with longsuffering, forbearing
one another in love.

*Ephesians 4:2, KJV*

Honesty time! Most of us manage to be patient
with the majority of the people in our lives. However, there are usually a couple of people who
cause us to struggle. Make a list of the three to four
people who test your patience. What are some
ways you can begin to approach them with
more forbearance?

"I tell you, love your enemies. Help and give without expecting a return. You'll never—I promise—regret it. Live out this God-created identity the way our Father lives toward us, generously and graciously, even when we're at our worst. Our Father is kind; you be kind."

*Luke 6:35–36, MSG*

This passage reminds us of God's unconditional generosity and kindness toward us. Complete this sentence: Because God was kind to me and loved me at my worst, I can try to . . .

But the Lord is faithful,
who will establish
you and guard you
from the evil one.

*2 Thessalonians 3:3, NKJV*

God is the one who protects us and guards us.
He is faithful to establish us. In the space to the
right, complete this thought: In my own life, I've
seen God be faithful in these ways . . .

First thing in the morning, she dresses for work, rolls up her sleeves, eager to get started. She senses the worth of her work, is in no hurry to call it quits for the day. She's skilled in the crafts of home and hearth, diligent in homemaking.

*Proverbs 31:17–19, MSG*

The womanly behavior described in Proverbs 31 includes being very hardworking. Take a moment to consider your own personal work ethic. Then, write down all the ways in which you show up for work, however you define it.

Enter into His gates with thanksgiving, And into His courts with praise. Be thankful to Him, and bless His name. For the Lord is good; His mercy is everlasting, And His truth endures to all generations.

*Psalm 100:4–5, NKJV*

It's easy to forget to praise the Lord and express our gratitude. To strengthen your praise muscles, try this exercise. In the space to the right, list the four to five qualities you most admire and appreciate about God. Then, take a few moments and tell Him how you feel.

Abigail flew into action. She took two hundred loaves of bread, two skins of wine, five sheep dressed out and ready for cooking, a bushel of roasted grain, a hundred raisin cakes, and two hundred fig cakes, and she had it all loaded on some donkeys.

*1 Samuel 25:18, MSG*

Have you ever had to fly into action to prepare a meal, welcome guests, or get your house in order? Describe a time when you had to act quickly to welcome guests. What did you have to do? How were your actions a blessing to others?

For You, Lord, are good,
and ready to forgive,
And abundant in mercy to
all those who call upon You.

*Psalm 86:5, NKJV*

What comes to mind when you think of God? Is He
a distant deity? A stern judge? A loving Father?
Complete this thought: When I think about God,
I see Him as . . .

And regardless of what
else you put on, wear love.
It's your basic, all-purpose
garment. Never be without it.

*Colossians 3:14, MSG*

Many of us women take great care making sure we look nice before starting the day. However, are you putting on love—our most essential garment? What if you asked God to clothe you in love each day? How might putting on love change you and the people you come in contact with?

A merry heart doeth good like a
medicine: but a broken spirit
drieth the bones.

*Proverbs 17:22, KJV*

A positive outlook can be a balm, but despair
can weigh us down. In the space provided, complete this thought: When I have a merry heart and
an optimistic approach, the rest of my world is
improved in these ways . . .

If it be possible,
as much as lieth in you,
live peaceably with all men.

*Romans 12:18, KJV*

On page 4, you reflected on the peacemakers you
know. What can you do to follow the examples of
these peacemakers in your life?

And let us not be
weary in well doing:
for in due season we shall
reap, if we faint not.

*Galatians 6:9, KJV*

It's easy to lose heart and grow weary. We all have days when we feel a little faint. But patience is also about perseverance. Make a list of some of the ways that you can keep yourself going today. Perhaps you can call a friend, go for a walk, or maybe put on some music and dance.

Do not forget to show
hospitality to strangers,
for by so doing some
people have shown hospitality
to angels without knowing it.

*Hebrews 13:2, NIV*

What might showing kindness and hospitality to
strangers look like in your life? What are two to
three practical ways you might begin to do this?

No test or temptation that comes your way is beyond the course of what others have had to face. All you need to remember is that God will never let you down; he'll never let you be pushed past your limit; he'll always be there to help you come through it.

*1 Corinthians 10:13, MSG*

Today's verse is like the trapdoor for sin. When you are tempted, you can call on God to get you out of harrowing situations. Detail some of the sins that are tempting and pulling at you right now. Pray over each one and invite God to give you a trapdoor to get away from these sins.

I can do all things through Christ
which strengtheneth me.

*Philippians 4:13, KJV*

How does Christ strengthen you and make you
more capable and more disciplined?

I thank my God every time
I remember you.

*Philippians 1:3, NIV*

When Paul thought about his friends in the
church at Philippi, he was thankful for them. And
he let them know it. Which two or three friends or
family members are you thankful for right now?
How might you let them know how much you
appreciate them?

The one who blesses others is abundantly blessed; those who help others are helped.

*Proverbs 11:25, MSG*

Describe a time when you were blessed after blessing or helping someone else.

She said, "May your servant find favor in your eyes." Then she went her way and ate something, and her face was no longer downcast.

*1 Samuel 1:18, NIV*

Sometimes, all you need to do is lay down your burdens, your pain, your bitterness. Take a few minutes to write out a prayer to the Lord. Honestly share your heart, your hurts, your burdens, and your concerns in your prayer.

There is no room in love for fear. Well-formed love banishes fear. Since fear is crippling, a fearful life—fear of death, fear of judgment—is one not yet fully formed in love.

*1 John 4:18, MSG*

There is something amazing about the power of love. Love drives out fear. How have you experienced this in your own life? How have you seen love defeat fear?

Thou wilt shew
me the path of life:
in thy presence is fulness
of joy; at thy right hand
there are pleasures forevermore.

*Psalm 16:11, KJV*

Even in the middle of sorrow, we can have joy—
almost unexplainable joy—in the Lord. The joy of the
Lord can give us strength and hope. In what ways
have you experienced the joy of the Lord recently?

Be careful for nothing;
but in every thing by prayer and
supplication with thanksgiving let
your requests be made known unto God.
And the peace of God, which passeth all
understanding, shall keep your hearts
and minds through Christ Jesus.

*Philippians 4:6–7, KJV*

Today's verses are a wonderful prescription for
peace. Suppose one of your family members was
worried and needed peace. Using the ideas from
Philippians, describe the way you would help this
person find peace.

Now may the God of patience and comfort grant you to be like-minded toward one another, according to Christ Jesus.

*Romans 15:5, NKJV*

This passage is about how we treat each other. Think about a time when someone treated you with great patience. What did they do, and how did it make you feel?

Whoever goes hunting for what is right
and kind finds life itself—glorious life!

*Proverbs 21:21, MSG*

What are you pursuing right now? Getting a raise
at work? Happiness? Have you thought about pursuing things like justice and kindness? In the space
to the right, complete this thought: If I began to
intentionally pursue justice and kindness in my life,
I can see my life changing in . . .

Because of the Lord's great love we are not consumed, for his compassions never fail. They are new every morning; great is your faithfulness.

*Lamentations 3:22–23, NIV*

It's possible you may wake up with regrets or insecurities or sadness about something that happened yesterday. But every day, you are given a chance to start anew with God's mercy and faithful love. In the space provided, finish this thought: Because the mercies of the Lord begin afresh and anew each morning, I . . .

For the grace of God has appeared that offers salvation to all people. It teaches us to say "No" to ungodliness and worldly passions, and to live self-controlled, upright and godly lives in this present age.

*Titus 2:11–12, NIV*

God's grace teaches us to say "No" to some things and to live with more self-control. What are two or three areas of your life where you could use more grace and self-control? In your diet, in your finances, in your relationships, or in some other area?

This is the day which the
Lord hath made; we will rejoice
and be glad in it.

*Psalm 118:24, KJV*

If you woke up and are breathing today, you can
be thankful. You are alive! The Bible encourages us
to be thankful for each day that God gives us. Use
the space to the right to finish this sentence: I'm
grateful for this new day because . . .

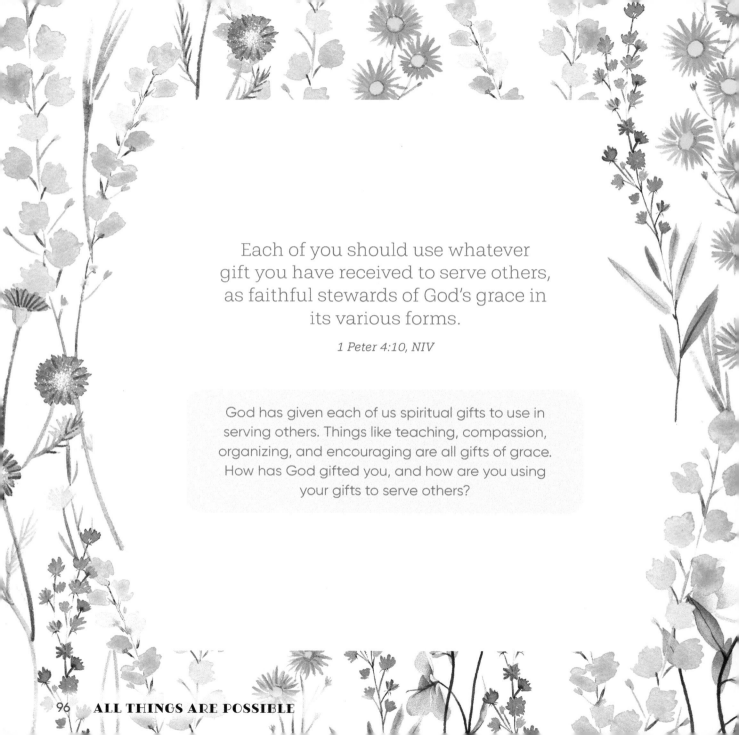

Each of you should use whatever
gift you have received to serve others,
as faithful stewards of God's grace in
its various forms.

*1 Peter 4:10, NIV*

God has given each of us spiritual gifts to use in
serving others. Things like teaching, compassion,
organizing, and encouraging are all gifts of grace.
How has God gifted you, and how are you using
your gifts to serve others?

In whom we have
redemption through his blood,
the forgiveness of sins, according
to the riches of his grace.

*Ephesians 1:7, KJV*

Not because of anything we have done, but
because of His blood, His grace, and His mercy, we
can be completely pardoned. Every debt erased—
past, present, and future. This is amazing news!
Have you experienced His forgiveness? How has His
forgiveness changed your life and your relationships
with others?

Let the morning bring me word of your unfailing love, for I have put my trust in you. Show me the way I should go, for to you I entrust my life.

*Psalm 143:8, NIV*

What is the first thing you think of when you wake up in the morning? What if you woke up intentionally thinking about the unending, unfailing, unbelievable love God has for us? How might resting in God's love make a profound difference in your work, your relationships, and your days?

O clap your hands, all ye people; shout
unto God with the voice of triumph . . .
Sing praises to God, sing praises: sing
praises unto our King, sing praises.

*Psalm 47:1, 6, KJV*

When was the last time you clapped and shouted
in joy and triumph to God? Why not do it now? In
the space to the right, list 10 to 15 reasons to offer
the Lord praise. Then, clap and shout them out to
Him. It may feel silly, but it will bring you joy!

Thou wilt keep him in
perfect peace, whose mind
is stayed on thee: because he
trusteth in thee.

*Isaiah 26:3, KJV*

Focus is everything in life. Where we fix our minds
and thoughts can greatly impact our days. How
might focusing on God bring more peace
into your life?

I pray to God—my life a prayer—and wait for what he'll say and do. My life's on the line before God, my Lord, waiting and watching till morning, waiting and watching till morning.

*Psalm 130:5–6, MSG*

Desperation in prayer is an amazing thing. When we come to the end of ourselves, we are able to sit at God's feet. Pouring everything out—every issue, problem, heartbreak—we watch and wait. What are you watching and waiting for today? Use this space to write out your prayer to the Lord as you wait.

The islanders showed
us unusual kindness.
They built a fire and welcomed
us all because it was
raining and cold.

*Acts 28:2, NIV*

Have you ever had someone show you
unusual kindness? What did they do?
How did this make you feel?

And we know that all things work together for good to those who love God, to those who are the called according to His purpose.

*Romans 8:28, NKJV*

Today's verse may be one of the most quoted verses of all time. In the simplest terms, we can be assured that God can work every single event, action, and issue in our lives for our good. How have you seen this principle to be true in your life?

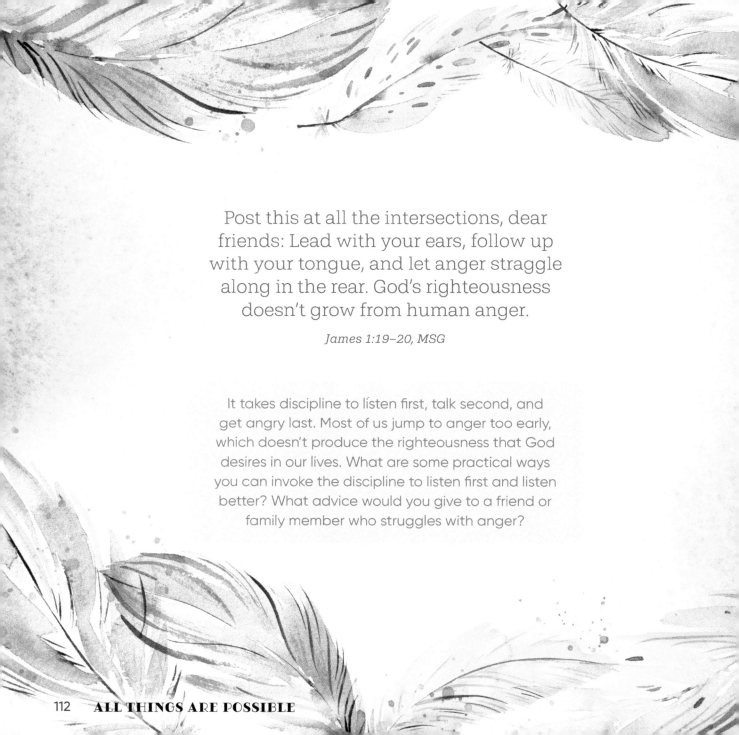

Post this at all the intersections, dear friends: Lead with your ears, follow up with your tongue, and let anger straggle along in the rear. God's righteousness doesn't grow from human anger.

*James 1:19–20, MSG*

It takes discipline to listen first, talk second, and get angry last. Most of us jump to anger too early, which doesn't produce the righteousness that God desires in our lives. What are some practical ways you can invoke the discipline to listen first and listen better? What advice would you give to a friend or family member who struggles with anger?

Be cheerful no matter what; pray all the time; thank God no matter what happens. This is the way God wants you who belong to Christ Jesus to live.

*1 Thessalonians 5:16–18, MSG*

How might you keep your cheer and spirit of thankfulness today even in the middle of your struggles?

So he got up from the supper table, set aside his robe, and put on an apron. Then he poured water into a basin and began to wash the feet of the disciples, drying them with his apron.

*John 13:4–5, MSG*

Sometimes, serving others can be uncomfortable, messy, or sobering. When was the last time you did something for others that was humbling or hard for you? Serving in a soup kitchen? Cleaning up trash in a local park? Visiting someone in a nursing home?

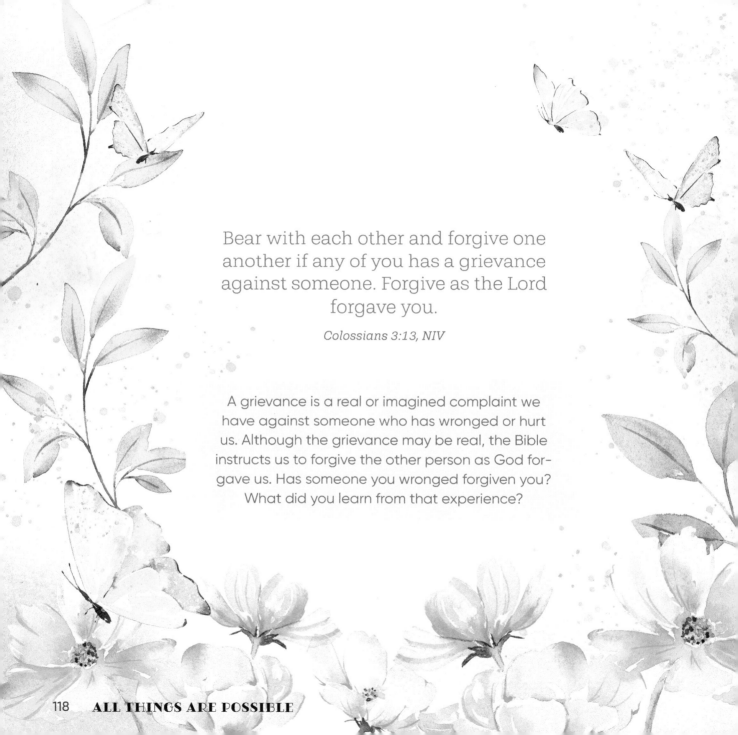

Bear with each other and forgive one another if any of you has a grievance against someone. Forgive as the Lord forgave you.

*Colossians 3:13, NIV*

A grievance is a real or imagined complaint we have against someone who has wronged or hurt us. Although the grievance may be real, the Bible instructs us to forgive the other person as God forgave us. Has someone you wronged forgiven you? What did you learn from that experience?

And he began to speak boldly in the synagogue: whom when Aquila and Priscilla had heard, they took him unto them, and expounded unto him the way of God more perfectly.

*Acts 18:26, KJV*

Aquila and Priscilla were mature believers who took the time to train and mentor Paul. Think about those in your life who have loved you enough to mentor you. List two or three of these people and describe how they have inspired you.

Now the God of hope fill you with all joy and peace in believing, that ye may abound in hope, through the power of the Holy Ghost.

*Romans 15:13, KJV*

The Apostle Paul prayed these words over the believers in the Roman church. Why not take the words of this verse and write a prayer for yourself and your family members?

These things I have spoken unto you, that in me ye might have peace. In the world ye shall have tribulation: but be of good cheer; I have overcome the world.

*John 16:33, KJV*

We live in a world filled with trouble and tribulations. But Jesus promised that we could be of good cheer in spite of all that is going on around us. Why do you suppose this is true?

A hot-tempered person stirs up conflict, but the one who is patient calms a quarrel.

*Proverbs 15:18, NIV*

We've all been in that moment when the conflicts arise. Getting angry only stirs things up more. But patience can calm and quiet a quarrel. How have you found this to be true in your dealings with other people?

It's criminal to ignore a
neighbor in need, but compassion
for the poor—what a blessing!

*Proverbs 14:21, MSG*

Compassion for the poor is a blessing to God, to
others, and to us. And it's not a hard thing for most
of us to do. How might you show more kindness to
the underprivileged in your community? Write out
several practical ways you might extend kindness
to someone less fortunate than yourself.

God is faithful, by whom you were called into the fellowship of His Son, Jesus Christ our Lord.

*1 Corinthians 1:9, NKJV*

To be dependable is to be steadfast, steady, and sturdy. You can be encouraged today that your God is dependable. He is faithful and reliable. How does this make you feel? In the space to the right, finish this sentence: I am grateful for the faithfulness of God because . . .

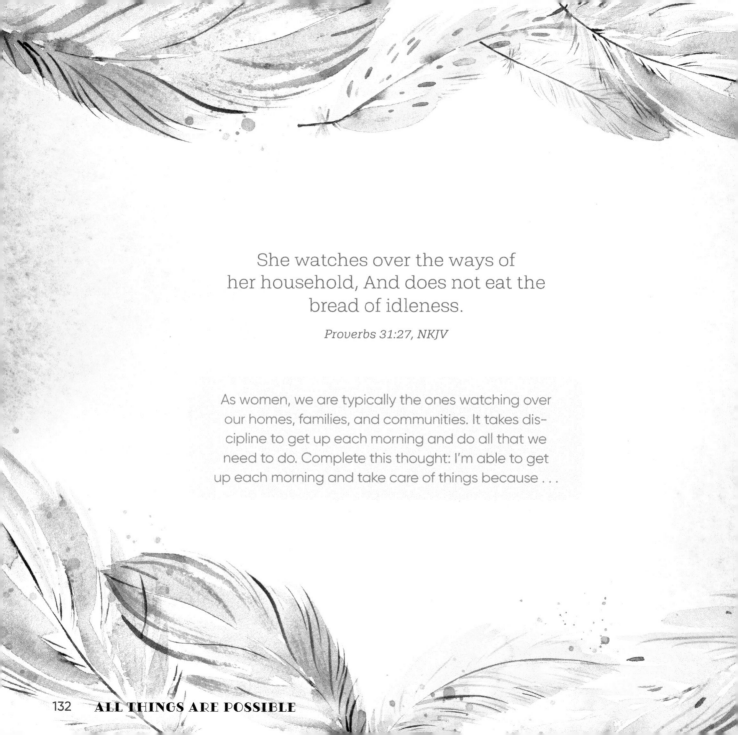

She watches over the ways of
her household, And does not eat the
bread of idleness.

*Proverbs 31:27, NKJV*

As women, we are typically the ones watching over
our homes, families, and communities. It takes discipline to get up each morning and do all that we
need to do. Complete this thought: I'm able to get
up each morning and take care of things because . . .

And Mary said: "My soul glorifies the Lord and my spirit rejoices in God my Savior, for he has been mindful of the humble state of his servant. From now on all generations will call me blessed."

*Luke 1:46–48, NIV*

When was the last time you wanted to sing praises because of something amazing God had done for you?

Now it happened as they went that He entered a certain village; and a certain woman named Martha welcomed Him into her house.

*Luke 10:38, NKJV*

We all know someone who makes us feel welcome; they always embrace you with open arms. Are you a welcoming person? In the coming days, what are some ways in which you can encourage your friends and family to feel like they can come into your home and enjoy community?

Keep a sharp eye out
for weeds of bitter discontent.
A thistle or two gone to seed can
ruin a whole garden in no time.

*Hebrews 12:15, MSG*

At times, life can truly be hurtful and can seem
unfair. But when we allow discontentment to hang
around and fester, it can lead to bitterness. How
can we keep an eye out for bitter discontentment?
What are some measures we can put in place to
protect ourselves from becoming angry or bitter?

And may the Master pour
on the love so it fills your lives and
splashes over on everyone around you,
just as it does from us to you.

*1 Thessalonians 3:12, MSG*

Have you ever been around someone who is so full
of God's love, grace, and kindness that it touches
everyone around them? It's refreshing! In what ways
have you been able to share God's love with those
around you?

For his anger endureth
but a moment; in his favour is life:
weeping may endure for a night, but
joy cometh in the morning.

*Psalm 30:5, KJV*

Sometimes, the brightest dawn comes after the darkest night. Maybe you've experienced this phenomenon in your own life. Reflect on a time when you found great joy after a long, hard period of weeping and despair. How did you get to that place of great joy?

I will both lay me down in peace,
and sleep: for thou, Lord, only
makest me dwell in safety.

*Psalm 4:8, KJV*

Many people struggle to rest because they can't
stop thinking or don't feel at peace. Tonight, write
down your worries before you go to bed, and invite
God to give you sweet peace as you sleep.

I remain confident of this: I will see the goodness of the Lord in the land of the living. Wait for the Lord; be strong and take heart and wait for the Lord.

*Psalm 27:13–14, NIV*

During those times when we lose heart, we can turn to these verses from Psalms and trust that we will eventually see God's goodness. He can give you the courage and strength to persist. Write a prayer inviting God to infuse you with courage and strength while you wait.

And let us not grow weary
while doing good, for in due season
we shall reap if we do not lose heart.

*Galatians 6:9, NKJV*

Someone may need your help today. Perhaps a
family in your church needs help paying their bills?
Or maybe a friend needs guidance? Write down
three to four people you believe to be in need. Pray
for them, and then reach out just to check in. If they
happen to mention a need, you can be a blessing
and offer them help.

There has never been the slightest doubt in my mind that the God who started this great work in you would keep at it and bring it to a flourishing finish on the very day Christ Jesus appears.

*Philippians 1:6, MSG*

As John Piper writes, "God is always doing 10,000 things in your life, and you may be aware of three of them." Record a brief timeline detailing the ways you have seen God work in your life. Note special events, great milestones, and answers to prayer. Thank God for how He has been at work in your life.

A person without self-control is like a house with its doors and windows knocked out.

*Proverbs 25:28, MSG*

Doors and windows on a house provide safety and boundaries. Just as our dwellings need enclosures, so, too, do our lives. It can take discipline to ensure that we're letting in things we need and keeping out things that don't serve us. Reflect on whether you are someone who has fully enclosed windows and doors. Are there places in need of better boundaries?

O give thanks unto the Lord; for he is good; for his mercy endureth forever.

*1 Chronicles 16:34, KJV*

We say, "God is good," but do we really believe it? And if we truly believe that God is good all the time, how might this impact our lives? Use the provided space to finish this sentence: Because I believe that God is good all the time . . .

After this, Jesus traveled about from one town and village to another, proclaiming the good news of the kingdom of God. The Twelve were with him, and also some women who had been cured of evil spirits and diseases: Mary (called Magdalene) from whom seven demons had come out; Joanna the wife of Chuza, the manager of Herod's household; Susanna; and many others. These women were helping to support them out of their own means.

*Luke 8:1-3, NIV*

Today, there are so many amazing ministries to support—both with prayer and with funds. What are some of the ways that you are supporting ministries and missions?

If we confess our sins,
He is faithful and just to forgive
us our sins and to cleanse us from
all unrighteousness.

*1 John 1:9, NKJV*

Take a moment to reflect on anything you may
have done (intentionally or unintentionally) that you
are asking God to forgive. Write those things down
and pray over each one, inviting Him to
absolve you of your guilt.

This is how God showed his love among us: He sent his one and only Son into the world that we might live through him. This is love: not that we loved God, but that he loved us and sent his Son as an atoning sacrifice for our sins.

*1 John 4:9–10, NIV*

Have you ever heard the words to the song "I Am Loved" by Gaither Vocal Band? "I am loved, I am loved / I can risk loving you / For the One who knows me best / Loves me most." If we absolutely know we are loved by God, how might that transform how we treat and relate to others?

Rejoice with them that do rejoice, and
weep with them that weep.

*Romans 12:15, KJV*

Have you ever had someone celebrate with you
when something amazing happened to you? Have
you experienced the compassion of a close friend
when you were struggling? How did it make you
feel to have another person rejoice or weep with
you? Consider how you can offer the same support
to someone you love in times of joy and sorrow.

Now the Lord of peace
himself give you peace
always by all means. The Lord
be with you all.

*2 Thessalonians 3:16, KJV*

When we spend time with the Lord, we can experience His peace, and our hearts are calmed and settled. Where and when do you personally feel God's peace in your life?

Whoever is patient has great understanding, but one who is quick-tempered displays folly.

*Proverbs 14:29, NIV*

When we are patient and slow to anger, we demonstrate wisdom and great understanding. But this is so hard! What are three to four practical ways you have discovered to help you slow down your anger?

"Do to others as you
would have
them do to you."

*Luke 6:31, NIV*

Here's a principle that stands the test of time. We treat others the way that we want to be treated. We give to others what we need: kindness, friendship, grace, and love. Make a list of ways you can offer kindness, friendship, grace, and love today.

"God is always on the alert, constantly
on the lookout for people who are totally
committed to him. You were foolish to
go for human help when you could have
had God's help. Now you're in trouble—
one round of war after another."

*2 Chronicles 16:9, MSG*

Think about a difficult time in your life when you put
your faith in God. What happened? What lesson
did you learn from relying on Him?

Brethren, I count not myself to have apprehended: but this one thing I do, forgetting those things which are behind, and reaching forth unto those things which are before, I press toward the mark for the prize of the high calling of God in Christ Jesus.

*Philippians 3:13–14, KJV*

No matter where we have failed in the past, we are encouraged to press on. Keep moving forward. Don't give up today. What are two to three situations that are holding you back today? How can you find ways to press on?

And let the peace of God rule in your hearts, to which also you were called in one body; and be thankful.

*Colossians 3:15, NKJV*

We are encouraged to allow God's peace to rule in our hearts and to be thankful to Him. Write a letter of gratitude to God today for the peace He brings into your heart. In what ways are you grateful to Him?

Hatred stirs up conflict, but love covers over all wrongs.

*Proverbs 10:12, NIV*

Look back over the most amazing relationships in your life. Did someone ever cover your wrongs and faults by offering you forgiveness through their love? How did that make you feel? Is there someone who deserves your love and forgiveness? What would that look like?

# RESOURCES

## BOOKS

*NLT Life Application Study Bible*. 2nd ed. Carol Stream, IL: Tyndale House, 2004.

Allen, Jennie. *Nothing to Prove: Why We Can Stop Trying So Hard*. Colorado Springs, CO: Waterbrook, 2017.

Batterson, Mark. *Double Blessing: How to Get It. How to Give It*. Colorado Springs, CO: Multnomah, 2019.

Elliot, Elisabeth. *Be Still My Soul: Reflections on Living the Christian Life*. Grand Rapids, MI: Revell, 2017.

Freeman, Emily P. *The Next Right Thing: A Simple, Soulful Practice for Making Life Decisions*. Grand Rapids, MI: Revell, 2019.

Goff, Bob. *Love Does: Discover a Secretly Incredible Life in an Ordinary World*. Nashville, TN: Thomas Nelson, 2012.

Redd, Melanie. *Live in Light: 5-Minute Devotions for Teen Girls*. Emeryville, CA: Althea Press, 2019.

Redd, Melanie. *Stepping Closer to the Savior*. Nashville, TN: CrossBooks, 2010.

Redd, Melanie, and Alison Tiemeyer. *Help! I Need Some Friends!: A 15-Day Friendship Challenge*. CreateSpace, 2016.

Snyder, John L. *Your 100 Day Prayer: The Transforming Power of Actively Waiting on God*. Nashville, TN: Thomas Nelson, 2011.

Strong, James. *The New Strong's Expanded Exhaustive Concordance of the Bible*. Nashville, TN: Thomas Nelson, 2010.

## APPS/WEBSITES

Bible Gateway. Accessed June 28, 2020. BibleGateway.com.

Bible Study Tools. Accessed June 28, 2020. BibleStudyTools.com.

First 5 app. Proverbs 31 Ministries. Accessed June 28, 2020. Proverbs31.org/study/first-5.

Piper, John. "God Is Always Doing 10,000 Things in Your Life." *Desiring God*. January 1, 2013. DesiringGod.org/articles/god-is-always-doing-10000-things-in-your-life.

# VERSE INDEX

## OLD TESTAMENT

# NEW TESTAMENT

# ACKNOWLEDGMENTS

Special thanks to my family for their support, prayers, encouragement, and patience during this project. Much appreciation as well to my prayer partners, Bible study group, and Blessing Counters Group. Also, I'm grateful to the wonderful staff at Callisto Media, especially to Joe Cho and Meera Pal. You guys are the best!

# ABOUT THE AUTHOR

**Melanie Redd** is a woman who loves to encourage, equip, train, and motivate other women. With her easy smile, warm personality, and positive outlook, she enjoys offering hope in all that she does.

Melanie wrote Sunday school curriculum and magazine articles for LifeWay Christian Resources before launching her own speaking, blogging, and writing ministry.

Melanie and her husband, Randy, live with their two amazing young-adult children and loveable Australian shepherd in Tennessee.

CPSIA information can be obtained
at www.ICGtesting.com
Printed in the USA
JSHW051121041220
9899JS00004BA/11

9 781647 399535

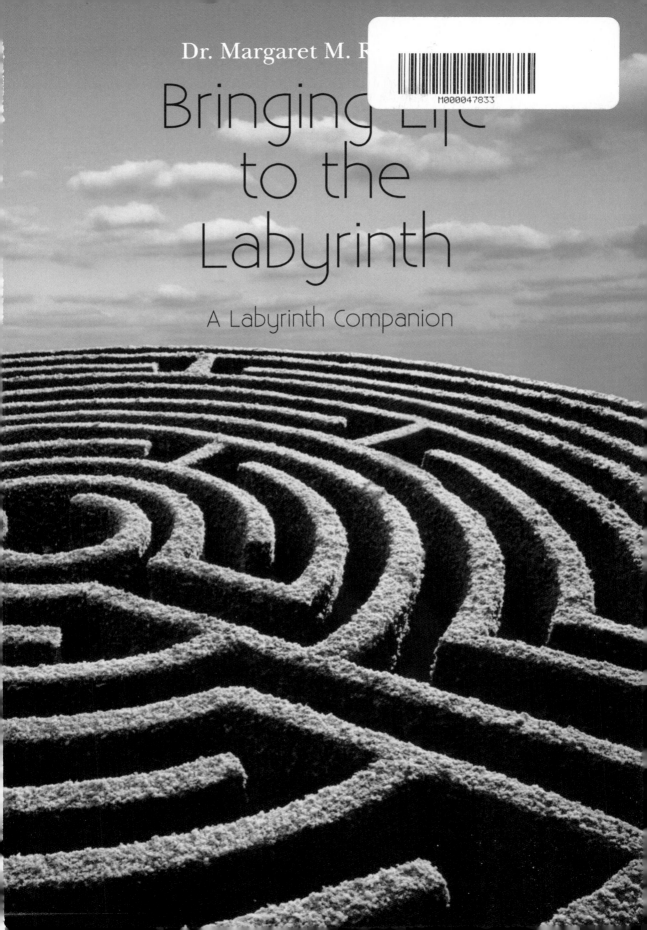

Dr. Margaret M. R.

# Bringing Life to the Labyrinth

## A Labyrinth Companion

# Image Descriptions

Title page: Modern garden labyrinth

Page 4: St Quentin, France

Page 7: Lucca, Italy

Page 8: Ely, England

Page 10: St Columba's Bay, Iona, Scotland

Page 14: New Harmony, Indiana, USA

Page 17: Canterbury England

Page 20 Valley Park, Copenhagen, Denmark

Page 24: Santa Rosa, California canvas labyrinth

Page 28: Mt. Baboquivari, Arizona, USA

Page 34: HRS Canvas Labyrinth USA

Page 37: Golden Door Spa, Arizona, USA

Page 40: Modern fountain labyrinth

Page 42: Greencastle, Indiana, USA

Page 46 Cumberton, Cambridgeshire, England

Page 47: Wooden finger labyrinth

Page 52: Grace Cathedral San Francisco, California , USA

Page 55: Maastricht, Netherlands

Page 57: Chartres Cathedral, France

Page 66: Plan of the labyrinth at Chartres Cathedral

Margaret M. Rappaport

# Bringing Life to the Labyrinth

## A Labyrinth Companion

ISBN: 0615966799
ISBN 13: 9780615966793

# Preface

As the modern world becomes increasingly complicated and people collect more facts to keep pace with life demands, we need to take time to recognize our fragile hold on what is possible beyond knowledge and action. Minds full of information and directed toward consumption are often blocked from the awareness that we can't know everything about the world, and we certainly don't know all there is to know about ourselves. Chronic focus on externals makes it easy to damage the ability to be conscious of endlessness and possibility within ourselves. Our imaginations and visions wither from the bombardment of stimulation that overwhelms us as we try to fit into the world. Spirituality and sensory awareness are wrenched away from us and sometimes lost in the swirl around us.

The labyrinth rests us. The practice of walking the labyrinth develops the ability to put aside distractions. It is a safe place where we can explore the inner world of feelings and tendencies as we take a fresh journey every time we walk. Walking the paths of the labyrinth, in quiet, we are reminded that the future is always in front of us and is never quite reached. When we return to the external world at walk's end, we bring along a sense of belonging to our own spirituality, and we feel more connected to other people. We are bolstered by this meditative exercise to renew our commitment to the Infinite, each according to our beliefs.

In the following I trust you will have a dependable companion to support your training and practice in walking the labyrinth. Please share your comments.   Licensed reproduction of images and photographs by Jeff Saward: info@labyrinthos.net

# Dedication

**For Julia Margaret Dobbins**
**For Charles Paul Dobbins**
**For Winona Louise Rappaport**

# Introduction

# Labyrinths Large and Small

With some certainty we can say the labyrinth symbol is more than four thousand years old. Jeff Saward wrote a thorough history of small labyrinths from many cultures in the ancient world. They were drawn on rock faces and pottery and, notably, coins. His work is well worth reading, not because what is known is conclusive, but because what is known about the labyrinth over time is important for understanding its meaning and use.

Over two thousand years hence, as the appearance of the labyrinth became more prevalent, its popularity continued to grow. Our certainty also increased about its importance in people's everyday experiences. For example, when Christianity pervaded the territories of the Roman Empire following the conversion of Emperor Constantine and the Council of Nicaea in 325 CE, the labyrinth symbol was absorbed into Christian philosophy, architecture, and domestic life. European labyrinths abounded during and after this period.

Today there is another astounding resurgence of interest in labyrinths, large and small. There are organizations, libraries, schools, and health centers focused on the labyrinth as a source of spiritual development, as well as health and wellness. A good resource for information on the current worldwide popularity of the labyrinth is www.labyrinthos.net.

Many recently built labyrinths are large enough for individuals or groups of people to walk. They are made like gardens and often are associated with towns and neighborhoods and other civic institutions. They are constructed indoors and outdoors. Workshops and facilitated walks are offered to guide people to the potential power of walking the labyrinth design.

Simultaneously, there is a brisk market in table labyrinths, finger labyrinths, and small labyrinths to look at and ponder. What do we do with the labyrinth when it is too small to walk? As the ancients did, we take contemplative exercise. We gaze at the design, and we think, feel, and imagine just as we do when we walk. The longer and more concentrated the looking, the greater the spiritual impact and the better our physical and mental health.

# What Are Labyrinths?

Labyrinths are pathways, often large enough to walk upon, that are shaped into twisting, turning designs. Christians have used them in spiritual practice for at least sixteen hundred years.

Labyrinths come in all shapes and sizes. Some are painted on surfaces or on a large piece of canvas, some are stone pathways laid in an open space or court-yard, some are mowed into grass on a lawn or in a park, while others come in a myriad of materials.

In today's world, Christians walk pathways of labyrinths for a variety of pur-poses: to pray or meditate, to find the quiet center of living, to facilitate calm and stillness in a hectic society, to find faithful clarity amid life's challenges and opportunities, to converse with God, to aid health and wellness, to heal from illness or trauma, to get in touch with the Holy Spirit, and much more.

An ongoing practice of labyrinth walking can be a celebrated discipline for Christians seeking an authentic life of balanced wholeness in which an intimate relationship with God and his faith community is sought and valued.

I want to let go of my personal objection to defining the labyrinth. Previous definitions are often confining and exist outside the imaginative, the meta-phorical, and the creative. I would rather my readers have an infinitely creative concept of the labyrinth. I'd rather encourage them to discover the labyrinth for themselves as they have their own experiences with it. I favor highlighting the mystery of the labyrinth as art, as cultural history, as spiritual inspiration.

Readers new to the labyrinth concept, however, may require a definition. They have good reasons for needing one. Wanting to share their interest in walk-ing the labyrinth they require ways to put their experiences into words. Often they have to start by stating an answer to the question, "What is a labyrinth?"

The most encompassing definition I can offer is the labyrinth is a walking meditation tool for personal and professional transformation and community building. It is used in sacred settings for spiritual growth, worship, and prayer. Labyrinth activities include presentations, unguided and facilitated contempla-tive walks, workshops, and breakout meetings during retreats and conferences. Labyrinths are used in supportive healing ceremonies for people challenged by physical and mental illnesses. Labyrinths help to focus and encourage people seeking health and wellness discipline. Labyrinth programs are sometimes tai-lored to people seeking to unleash their creative potential. Labyrinths can serve as a core feature of a community, becoming a meeting place and a place of respite in a busy environment.

There are as many reasons for and uses of the labyrinth as people can envision. We are ready to relate to walking the labyrinth in many different ways. It is a providential resource for all of us to use and cherish.

# What Led Me to This Place?

I've been thinking about "bringing life to the labyrinth" as a theme for facilitating people's meditative walks. It occurred to me recently that the labyrinth is particularly suited for pondering where we are in our lives and how we got to this place. All of us have found our lives to be far from where they should have been. We all have experienced the realization that our lives are not exactly what we wanted them to be. Most of us, however, give little time and attention to what decisions or circumstances led us to the place where we now find ourselves. Often, even less attention is given to growth and change, as we are busy with the demands of simply living our lives as they have turned out.

In the labyrinth, we sense a "place-less-ness" that clears our way to take a fresh look at life. In the labyrinth it doesn't matter how much money we have, how healthy a body we have, how nice a home we own, or how intelligent and clever we are. Status and many of the identifying characteristics we possess are left at the gate. In this place for a period of time, we are spontaneously let loose to create new perspectives. We may not be able to fully transform our lives, but we surely can discover the means to reform choices and behaviors for our own benefit.

As we walk the labyrinth, we also have the opportunity to acknowledge the important connections we have to other people on our life's journey. For some of us, our relationships are a big part of why we are where we are in our lives. None of us lives life alone. Whether we see ourselves as rugged individuals who control our destinies or compliant followers in families and communities, in the labyrinth our views of ourselves can be reshaped, if we desire.

# The Labyrinth Is a Thin Place

Let's consider what makes a "thin place" before we look at the way the labyrinth fits the description. The term "thin place," like the name "labyrinth," has ancient origins in many different cultures. The Celtic people used it to indicate mesmerizing places in the environment. They suggested that heaven and earth were only three feet apart, but in thin places that distance was shorter. Thin places are deep, however, and they afford us glimpses of transcendence, infinite time and space, the divine.

Early Christians viewed a thin place as a meeting place between the material world and the spiritual realm, where the eternal seeped through to the physical world and thereby to us. For them, thin places were often sacred spaces in basilicas and churches. Mircea Eliade, author of *The Sacred and the Profane*, discusses the religious context of thin places: "Some parts of space are qualitatively different from others." Thin places transform us, and we become more fully ourselves having been inspired by being in them.

Buddhists tell us that sacred spaces get us in touch with "suchness." While these places may not be beautiful or tranquil, as we might expect, they usually jolt us into fresh ways of thinking and feeling. We find within ourselves new, unanticipated sensations and perceptions that stir us. We become quiet, relaxed, and beguiled.

Perhaps you can see the comparisons emerging. You might realize that you can plan for encountering thinness. You need not wait to discover thin places, although that will always happen. You can choose to increase the opportunity to find this solitary experience. I recall the Apache proverb "Wisdom sits in places." Some or many of us may find wisdom in the labyrinth. One person's walk in the labyrinth will not be the same as another's, of course, but often when we walk together, we enhance each other's awareness of what we seek from our time on the spiraling pathway.

As usual, have no expectations and don't follow another's style. Simply let loose, unmask, lose your bearings, and find new ones on your walk in the labyrinth.

# A Not-So-Modern Human Need for the Labyrinth

Origins of the labyrinth remain a mystery. Although these designs date back five thousand years and examples are found throughout the world in many diverse cultures, there is no definitive explanation for the labyrinth. From the earliest examples in Europe on rocks, tiles, pottery, and stone and wooden tablets to the reemergence of the labyrinth today, the only thing known for certain is the importance of the labyrinth for people.

Labyrinths are designs featuring a single spiral path that leads from the outside to a center space. Walking in or on the labyrinth follows the path to the center and back again to the outside. In the western hemisphere, Native American tradition features the labyrinth as the medicine wheel and in "Man in the Maze" designs on baskets. In northern Europe and throughout the Roman Empire, Celtic people called the labyrinth the "never-ending circle," and it appears often and in random places. In Judaism, the labyrinth is referred to as the Kabala and is thought to have mystical power. Not all labyrinths lie on the ground to be walked, but when they are made of earth or stone, they are usually used for walking. The labyrinth, however, is a compelling example of artistic expression as it enhances human environments, whether seen on doors, wall plaques, and gates, or on inside floors or the ground outside.

Walking the labyrinth or seeing it displayed may help people feel centered and more peaceful in living their lives. Some describe this as a clarity that promotes a connection between the body, mind, and spirit. People also describe it as a quieting of thoughts or of having an innovative, meditative state of mind. Others say walking the labyrinth fosters insight and self-reflection. Many wellness advocates say practice in walking the labyrinth reduces the stress of life and opens space within people for celebration and happiness despite external circumstances.

During the Middle Ages in Europe, the labyrinth design started to appear in churches, on village greens, and even on offshore islands as far north as the Arctic region. Now again, in the twenty-first century, communities of people are building labyrinths because of a resurgence of interest. In the United States, labyrinths can be found in parks, churches and cathedrals, schools, medical centers, spas, cemeteries and memorial parks, retreat centers, and in many yards and on other personal property. The materials these labyrinths are made from are as varied as their locations and uses. The central distinction, however, is that people are building them and gathering in and on them for a purpose that, apparently, reflects a human need to meet in concert to follow a meaningful path.

# Is the Labyrinth Useful?

You may have heard the labyrinth called a tool. I have used this idea to guide people in understanding the reasons we walk the labyrinth in a variety of settings. I've also suggested that the labyrinth is a metaphor. I have asked people to consider the labyrinth an imaginary and mystical space. I've told people that artists and gardeners claim the labyrinth as part of their work in the world. Obviously, the labyrinth can be seen in many different ways.

What does it mean to use the name "tool" in describing the labyrinth? I think the labyrinth is a "tool" because it is something that can be adapted at whatever level might be appropriate for those who seek to benefit from it.

Walking the labyrinth can be an exercise in meandering relaxation. It can just as well facilitate concentration or aid clarification regarding some issue or problem. It affords contemplation time without interruption. It can be an attractive meeting place for purposeful activity.

In sacred settings the labyrinth can be used as a meditation tool that tunes prayer and, more broadly, spiritual growth. Walking the labyrinth clears the mind of extraneous and everyday matters like a broom, a mop, or, more efficiently, a vacuum cleaner would do.

In secular settings, walking the labyrinth focuses the mind like a camera or microscope. When I've asked groups to free-associate, thinking of the labyrinth as a tool to use for transforming their experience, they offer wrench, hammer, drill, screwdriver, and other common mechanical tools. Often their imaginations take them in an electronics direction. The bottom line: the idea that the labyrinth can be useful is familiar to people.

Finally, seeing the labyrinth as a tool gives it a more everyday appeal. The easier it is to feel comfortable walking the labyrinth, the more often people will seek out the benefits of doing it. Responding to the appeal and popularity and usefulness of labyrinths is bound to motivate people to include them among life's best things as they have proven to be for thousands of years.

# Power in the Patterns of the Labyrinth

Let's look at the pattern referred to as the Chartres-style labyrinth as our example, we are immediately struck by the patterns we see. There are six rosettes that make up the center. There are lunations, or small half circles, around the outside edge. As we begin to walk, we experience the lines that outline the lanes we are following. We walk the lanes into the center and walk out from the center following the same pathway. There is one single lane, but there seem to be many lanes. This spiraling pathway is 860 feet in length.

The patterns both expand and limit our choices as we walk. They give us the sense that our steps count for something because the slow walking changes our breathing, not just our pace. Walking the spiraling lane, we become aware of "things changing" and of "transformation" as we can't see ahead or behind. We are just on the path, and we turn inward. Time seems to expand.

Every walk in the labyrinth is a journey of self-discovery. Every walk in the labyrinth is a connection with people here and now and in times past. Every walk in the labyrinth connects us more fully to ourselves and to people in hundreds of diverse cultures.

Another set of patterns within our human bodies may be the inspiration for the sense of connection to self and to others. For example, the winding lanes resemble the cerebral spirals of our brains, as well as the structure and motion of our gastrointestinal tract.

Spirals in nature abound, and we may recognize them as we walk the labyrinth. We may remember Fibonacci spiraling sequences in roses, pinecones, and daisies, and that we are dazzled by them. In shells and vines and galaxies, we sense connections, convergences, and coincidences in our experiences in the labyrinth.

As we walk the labyrinth, awareness of the myriad spiraling in nature and the similarities in patterns we experience in our bodies leads us to a greater understanding of the meaning of images, ideas, and feelings as we live our lives individually and in communities.

# A Single Path

The most striking difference between a labyrinth and a maze is the path. The single pathway into and out of the labyrinth encourages us to enter with reverence because we recognize that the end is the same as the beginning. Only life experience at its most fundamental can be characterized that way. That awareness makes us focus. We are urged forward without regard for choices or direction. The beginning will eventually become the end, although there is no way to know how long the walk will take. There is also no way to prepare for what thoughts, feelings, images, or whisperings of the heart we might find along the way.

In a maze, there is mystery and fun. Direction requires discernment and making good choices if we are to enjoy the experience. Whether walking, running, or hiding in a maze, our actions are not prescribed or predicted by the pattern. Solving the maze takes our attention. The maze distracts us from the rest of our concerns. It encourages us to play. All human cultures construct mazes, just as they create labyrinths, but the purposes of each type of garden or structure are not similar.

People seem to require the renewal we get as we walk in labyrinths and wander in mazes. Time spent in them relieves the urgency of living. Each is a means of learning about us. Each offers encouragement to the seeker, the weary, the puzzled, and the unwell. Each changes our frame of mind, our behaviors, and our spirits.

The labyrinth urges reflection and, for some, meditation and prayer. The maze urges relaxation, freedom, and play. They both call us away from life as usual for a period of time. We benefit from listening to those calls to be well and fully human. Some of us believe we should pray often, and laugh and play more, because it's the way to love one another.

# Structure:
# Meaning and Use

# Try Something New: Walk the Labyrinth

Personally, I don't entirely endorse the never-ending quest to try something new or exciting or even creative. Living a rewarding life in a busy world is difficult enough without an overload of choices and activities that demand time and energy, in my view. So it's exceptional that I would ask others to consider walking the labyrinth on a regular basis. Let me assure you of the benefits.

There is a spirit of active, imaginative adventure that derives from a walk in the labyrinth. The adventure may be internal, but it is deeply exciting. It is a kind of ingenuity that motivates new outlooks and new goals. It is ingenious play that spontaneously explores novelty in the corners of living. It is an alternative form of exercise that engages mind and body in fresh ways. It is magically habit forming!

Walking the labyrinth opens doors to more robust wellness. It alters attitude. It uplifts mood. It clarifies perspective. It calms feelings. It stretches the muscles and soothes the nervous system. There is some recent research that suggests that this type of walking meditation results in positive changes in gene expression. All of this may help explain the sudden popularity of labyrinths and the practice of walking in them.

Trying something new is not always successful, as we all know. Trying out the labyrinth, however, doesn't require an investment in equipment. Walking the labyrinth usually occurs in relative privacy. Silence often prevails, so critical comments of others are at a minimum. Manuals and lesson books are non-existent. Abundance, enthusiasm, and self-love are plentiful and available on demand in the labyrinth. Wisdom, both secular and sacred, is accessed as we encounter the challenges and risks of our personal experiences in walking the labyrinth. Well, in this case, new may be better.

Whoever you are and wherever you are in your life's journey, you are invited to explore walking the labyrinth with me. If you are seeking a resource for inspiration, some new ideas about the power of labyrinths to enlighten and heal, or simply a place for support through whatever the changes and chances of life bring you, there is space for you in the labyrinth.

We who are walking the labyrinth are a growing community in the United States and in many other parts of the world. The ease and practicality of walking encourage all ages to get involved but are especially attractive for people in their sixties and seventies. Being in the labyrinth offers us a wide range of opportunities to learn or relearn about each other and ourselves. Walking the labyrinth engages the whole person and the entire group of participants in a meaningful activity that has remarkable consequences. The benefits of walking the labyrinth cannot be overstated.

I invite you to get to know the labyrinth better. I will share the various reasons for walking the labyrinth for wellness, stress reduction, spiritual growth, solace, and the development of wisdom. You will also read about the history and design of labyrinths, including why they have particular structures and are made of various materials. I will offer virtual facilitated walks that you and groups can take into familiar labyrinths near you.

# Bringing Life to the Labyrinth

Walking the labyrinth becomes devotional when it is frequent and purposeful. Often that doesn't mean having an agenda or a set of goals for each walk. It means being open to new thoughts and feelings, whatever they may be and however they may come to you as you walk. Bringing your life to the labyrinth with an attitude of hopefulness and trust is freeing. It is also courageous. Making time and space in your life for growth, renewal, insight, and transformation is risky!

Walking the labyrinth is a place to rely on for inspiration, which is why it lends itself to devotional practice. Like other opportunities for prayer, worship, and meditation, walking the labyrinth creates an environment for transcending, uplifting, and enriching life. A sense of abundance pervades every walk. Enthusiasm for fresh possibilities and unimagined potentials flows through and in and around every walk, every time.

Devotion to walking the labyrinth has an obvious effect. It invites with regularity the spiritual, the divine presence into your ordinary experience. Walking the labyrinth becomes a pilgrimage, a journey toward personal expansion and knowledge of God. Walking the labyrinth promotes a greater awareness of the meaning and purpose of your individual life in relation to God's plan for humanity.

My personal experience after eleven years of devotion to walking the labyrinth has led me to author a book. *Bringing Life to the Labyrinth* shares images of labyrinths, discusses mystical and wellness uses of labyrinths, and brings together ideas and concepts of the contemporary importance of labyrinths. It is written to be a companion to walking the labyrinth. It seeks to connect people to one another in their devotion. Its resolve is to pilot the formation of a labyrinth community. I am humbly grateful for the inspiration that underlies "bringing life to the labyrinth."

# Guidelines for Walking a Labyrinth

It's a good idea to look at some guidelines for walking a labyrinth. Don't think, first of all, that there is a right way or a wrong way. There are guidelines, not requirements, and the only purpose in following those is that one wants to walk the labyrinth. People need not walk perfectly, nor are they expected to perform in exact ways. To **walk freely** is the point and the first guideline.

The patterns that make up a labyrinth require that people do what comes naturally when they meet in the labyrinth. They step aside or around each other with or without acknowledgment. This casualness comes easily to most people because it mimics walking on trails or on roads and sidewalks. When people know each other and are walking together, they greet each other in whatever way seems appropriate at the time. People are always allowed to be alone on their walks. Therefore, **spontaneity** is the second guideline.

Walking the labyrinth is self paced, not prescribed by others or dictated by the forms and shapes of the patterns. Walkers follow the pace that suits their own inward and outward needs. Some people walk very slowly and even stop at various points. Others prefer dance-like movements through different parts of the labyrinth. At various ages, people often show distinct styles of movement during a walk. The third guideline is to **be ourselves**. Following a personal flow enhances the experience of metaphor and imagination.

Think of the labyrinth as a tool to help people nurture the spirit, the body, and the mind. All of us know instinctively how to use the tool. No need for self-conscious poses and attitudes, just go for the walk and be encouraged.

# A Metaphor for Life's Journey

When you stand at the entrance to the labyrinth, one thing is certain. Beginning the walk calls for a self-expressive response of one kind or another. Some people approach this moment with resolve, even eagerness. Others hesitate and look around for cues. This describes those people who show up for a walk. Some never expect to walk and withdraw from trying because of misgivings. Walking the labyrinth prompts asking questions of oneself. Walking the labyrinth opens a space within that requires a response to those questions.

Response is an interesting word. The Latin verb *respondere*, to engage oneself or to promise, shows us the meaning of "responding to our own questions." Walking the labyrinth is the epitome of promise and engagement for everyone who is earnest about his or her experience.

As we walk the labyrinth, we make a requisite act of trust. We breathe deeply and mark a new point in the intimacy with ourselves. We ready ourselves for ideas and insights about living now, in the past, or in the future. We take on the walk as a metaphor of our life's journey. We release the limits of description and explanation, and embrace the events and mysteries that move us. We seek the heart of ourselves. We recognize that the response we make is spontaneous. The response is freely mine, and it is mine alone. We respond to ourselves because "we feel like it."

Some of us think this is a wonderful way to live our lives. Our responses in the labyrinth are really quite simple - to be ourselves, uncluttered, without calculating all the ifs, ands, buts, howevers, and maybes that punctuate our lives. No need for qualifiers and clarifiers, our value and worth are determined by our inner honesty. Our spirits are uplifted, and we know ourselves better.

# An Imaginary Vantage Point

To become deeply involved in the spiritual practice of walking the labyrinth is a simple matter for people. The desire to walk comes first. Then, predictably, we experience ourselves as figures on the pathways. Next, we recognize others, real or imagined, who may be walking with us. Slowly, as we walk over and over for a period of time, we go beyond the limits of our personal outlook. We begin to perceive everything as a wonderful whole. We identify with as many people as possible. We seek and search for an imaginary point from which we can expand our vision as much as possible. The vistas of human spiritual life spontaneously present themselves.

These steps along the path into and out of the labyrinth don't happen according to a predetermined schedule. Walks may number in the hundreds before a sense of meaningfulness emerges. Years may go by before time changes our usual outlook. Transformation won't be hurried, and it can't be faked. Walking the labyrinth doesn't leave room for posturing or pretending. Spiritual practice demands a space and time of its own.

As we practice, entering the center of the labyrinth encourages us to take the time we need to exercise our imaginations. What are our sensations? What do we perceive? What is happening to us in this particular surrounding? What do we see and hear? What in our thoughts and feelings is clarified? Is walking really a prayer?

Holy Scripture tells us many stories of the kind of expansion of spirit that occurs when human beings strive to encounter God. The stories recount that God is also searching for us. These experiences occur in a variety of settings, although the time and place are always made sacred. Perhaps the labyrinth can be viewed as a space that humans and God have agreed upon as having the potential to be sacred. The labyrinth looks and feels unique, as it has for centuries. In churches, especially, it shines forth as poetic, artistic, and it draws people forward onto its pathways and into its center. It's not an impossible idea to think of the labyrinth as an imaginary vantage point where human spirit meets divine glory, is it?

# Playing an Infinite Game in the Labyrinth

Theologian James Carse, a professor at New York University, and the author of *Finite and Infinite Games*, identified two types of games. Finite games are familiar and infinite games are novel. Finite games end. They have a winner and a loser, even when only one person plays. I'm sure you can list all of the ball games and card games and puzzles that are finite games. Infinite games, however, are games that don't end. They are games that stay in play from time to time and from place to place. These games are observable if you are prepared to look for them, but describing them is difficult.

Walking the labyrinth is an infinite game. As long and as often as we walk, it never has an ending. When our current walk concludes, we are aware that there will be a next time, and the labyrinth will always be the same. We may not be the same, and the walk won't be the same, but the space will be the same welcoming shape it always is. Our experience will be different and familiar at the same time. One walk is in some ways like another, yet in most ways it is unique.

Walking the labyrinth gets us in touch with the infinite as the spiral paths won't yield to our sense of time management and control. We are unable to predict our pace and our thoughts and feelings as we walk. Often we have an awareness that time has slowed down or sped up. We feel detached from everyday life, yet we find ourselves in the insights that come to us.

The infinite game of walking the labyrinth doesn't have an outcome. It begins and continues. We pick up unconscious currents that shape us. We may experience transcendence from the ordinary without fearing loss of control. It is an infinite game that is played to lose our usual sense of security. As an infinite game, it is played to embrace freedom. The labyrinth is an infinite game because it is played to find out, to find ourselves, to go beyond.

# Personal/Professional Transformation

# Walking the Labyrinth for Personal Transformation

Signals from just outside our ordinary awareness are faint. We can barely recognize them. Personal change is nearby, but rarely are the messages blaring. We may begin with thoughts and feelings, but we have to make more of an effort to connect with our inklings and intuitions. We have to let go of preoccupations with the whys and wherefores of everyday life. We have to spend some time being receptive to the unconscious, the macrocosmic mind, and the artistic mind that creates images. Wishing to transform some part of us requires imagination and a mobilizing of personal creativity.

We may be seeking education or guidance. We might want our everyday life and relationships to be different but can't envision them. Our sexuality may be puzzling. Our ambitions might seem out of reach, and still they don't let us alone. A person's progress isn't determined by his or her DNA, and so we constantly need updating. That is easy to say, but it's not very easy to make time and design a place for doing it. Transformation is especially hard because it demands that we take a different route from those we use to solve problems or design our plans. If we desire personal change, we have to take the risk of being inactive and quiet and wait for what occurs to us. The two outstanding risks lie in not anticipating or liking our own creative outcomes and having nothing occur to us for a long time. And, furthermore, it's something we have to do for ourselves. We can make use of the labyrinth as a meditative tool. Walking the labyrinth for personal transformation centers our attention and presents the ambience for reflection. It is amenable to secular or spiritual attitudes; therefore, it is personally customized. The labyrinth is a secure physical place to let images flow slowly or fast and furiously because it contains and embraces us. We are free to wander in body, mind, and spirit. Whether we meet each other, the divine spirit, or just ourselves, we can be assured that what happens will have meaning and will be important. A flash of insight, a sunlit image, a whispered sound, or a breeze might convey a treasure for us. Another's smile, a hug from someone passing us on the pathway, or a pleasant glance across the labyrinth may offer all the support we need to confirm our transformations.

# The Luxury of Quiet Thinking

What if every time you walked the labyrinth you accepted a sense of power to change the world for the better? What if I told you that your imagination could be so stimulated by the experience of walking the labyrinth that you could make change happen? Would you believe me?

Bear with me, for miracles large and small do abound, and people are often the catalysts. The imaginative process released while walking the labyrinth is real. It comes as a truly luxurious experience. It grows like magic as you practice. The more you do it, the more progress is made in hope and ideals and wisdom. That result alone is enough to change the world for the better. What would the world be like if many people believed in this consequential change and began in earnest to walk the labyrinth?

Let's imagine that we want to change the way our culture encourages us to degrade our environment or promote health crises through poor nutrition decisions. Suppose we take the time to center these ideas in our mind. Then let us take them into the labyrinth and walk with them. Enjoy the luxury of quietly thinking during a slow and rhythmic walk on a single pathway. Try to feel the importance of unspoiled nature. Try to aspire to healing, health, and happiness in your own life. Espouse to the community the possibility for positive change in interacting with the environment. Unleash the wonder of dynamic healthy behaviors. When you step out at the end of your walk, breathe deeply and exhale luxuriously.

As we enjoy the luxury of walking the labyrinth, we embrace the age-old human skill of freeing our imaginations. We bring poetry to life, and that's a change from the ordinary.

# Practice Patience as You Walk

Each time we enter the labyrinth an opportunity presents itself. The thought may come in different ways to each of us, but it often contains a question. What is in my heart? What are the things that are unresolved in my feelings? What will I experience today since I can't look at everything in my life in a single walk? How can I trust myself to find meaning and answers to my most pressing questions?

When I facilitate a group walk, I suggest to people that they try to embrace, even love their questions. Don't search for the answers; live the questions! The point is to live now, here not there. Live the questions, and be present with your quest. Think of your questions as though they are spoken in a language you don't understand or barely hear. Tell yourself that answers would not be recognized if you got them. You are still in a questioning phase of your life journey. You're at the start or at some middle point, not the finish, and that may be a reason you're walking the labyrinth.

Walking the labyrinth is an exercise in valuing the "gradual." It raises our awareness that, without noticing it, we live our way into our choices and decisions. If we are patient with ourselves and honor our questions, we will, perhaps, find meaningful answers. The resolutions may be near or far, but they are often in our future. We can't know that place and time. We must patiently wait for it.

Walking the labyrinth encourages us, of course, to access our spiritual resources for guidance in our questioning. We may not, however, get answers but only more deeply felt questions. Be patient. Just as the walk requires an attitude of patience (you will eventually walk out of the space!), so living well and happy is best done in a spirit of practiced patience.

Labyrinth walks are always a friendly reminder of our loves, our limits, and our lifelong need for learning. Try to live and love the gradualness of a labyrinth walk. It perfects the practice of patience, which benefits our journeys.

# I Thrive by Walking the Labyrinth

I sometimes think I was born in a library! Words ignite my imagination and pique my curiosity; reading is one of my greatest pleasures. Writing about the labyrinth has become one of my most satisfying achievements.

In preparing a post for my blog, I got lost in juxtaposing two words that rhyme and signify much of my life's journey. They are "strive" and "thrive." Consulting a thesaurus, I enjoyed the related words for thrive: flourish, prosper, bloom, blossom, and succeed. Related words for strive were very different and more complicated: struggle, make every effort, attempt, try hard, and do all you can. Both words, however, seem to proclaim that in my life I should pull out all the stops. Whether I am striving or thriving, I should hear a boom!

I chose "thrive" to take into a walk in the labyrinth. Those related words seemed better suited to the mood that settles over me when I walk there. Almost from the outset, I feel growth and renewal beckoning. A spirit of joyousness surrounds me. I sense a divine presence urging me to connect with all creation. Deep gratitude flows inside me. I thrive to the fullest while I walk.

In my busy working life, there are many opportunities to strive. Those offer distinct satisfaction. Professional activities that include a variety of contacts with people are a source of wonder. I look forward to each day. Opportunities to stop and appreciate how striving and thriving are linked in my life, however, have to be shaped; the labyrinth's very structure reminds me to do it!

Commitment to walking the labyrinth guarantees I will make the time and space in my routines to pause my striving in order to spend my life beautifully and "thrive."

# My Thoughts as I Walk

As I walk the labyrinth, it is sometimes hard to sort out what's what. Although I feel the meaning of being in this space, and I have many reasons for walking here, I am quiet but still unsettled. It's hard to separate what inspires me from what dispirits me. Distinguishing the high spirits from the false spirits occupies my thoughts as I slowly walk the spiraling path.

The labyrinth is a symbol of centeredness, and it puts me into greater awareness of my spirit. St. Augustine famously said, *"Solvitur ambulando"* ("It is solved by walking"), and I agree. I walk the labyrinth by following the path inward and then outward from side to side. It helps me understand where I have been and where I may go.

I walk the labyrinth with other people. I celebrate with them the winding pattern that connects our stories and our life journeys. I imagine the coincidences that have brought us together. We all have something to learn from this connectedness. I find the sense of community uplifting.

# Walking the Labyrinth for Professional Transformation

I've been fortunate to facilitate meditative walks in a labyrinth as breakout sessions at major conferences for professionals in health care and in aviation. I've had a learning curve to discover ways to approach professional development in these two unique contexts. I would like to share a general perspective from my experiences.

A majority of health-care personnel have some knowledge and sometimes familiarity with labyrinths. Physicians, nurses, and medical technicians encounter them in hospital settings, nursing facilities, and churches. Community labyrinths sometimes figure prominently in their experience. They feel somewhat comfortable conceding to a labyrinth walk focused on change and bringing new perspectives to their professional roles.

Aviation professionals, most often pilots and mechanics, do not initially appear at ease with walking the labyrinth as a way to promote professional growth. That doesn't mean they are uneasy; it's only that they find themselves in a novel context for exploring professional transformation. They require some preparation to benefit from walking the labyrinth. Happily, the new vocabulary and community spirit usually please them.

Professional transformation for anyone is a goal to expand work skills. It starts with intention. Although it may be difficult and may need prompting, we contemplate letting go of the professional roles we have learned and repeated, looking at the jobs we are used to doing and thinking of ourselves otherwise, examining the status and delight in what we have achieved, and questioning ourselves as the leader others admire. Transformation anticipates that we might reinvent, even reenvision ourselves. Why would we want to do that? Some of the outcomes include setting new work goals for ourselves that are more rewarding; analyzing our connections to and the inspiration we get from our work life renews our energy to do our work; and reflecting on ourselves as professionals contributes to an overall sense of self-esteem. Why, if given the opportunity, wouldn't we take the time to walk the labyrinth as an impetus to achieve these transformations?

## Serenity

"When the mind, divided and torn, is drawn into so many and such weighty matters, where can it return to itself, so as to recollect itself"...? Pope Gregory the Great was guiding us to prayer in sacred spaces by acknowledging our desperation. He was pointing us to our inner spirit of serenity that comes as a gift from God and is always offered to us. Only our choice to access it is limited, never limited is the potential to experience it.

Walking the labyrinth encourages us to bravely link our human desperation and our God-given sense of serenity. Attaching ourselves to God's presence and promise in prayerful contemplation becomes an active, heartfelt choice. As we retreat from specific daily cares into meditation on our walk, we encounter strengthening thoughts and feelings. Desperation may frankly be seen as an all-too-human "sickness" that comes as a result of emotions that have no ready spot in our life situation. Serenity may be recognized as courage, a cardinal virtue manifested by many others in times of peril. We may reflect on our heroic but limited capacities for human struggle. We may humbly enlist God's power through the wisdom and revelation of scripture.

Changes in our perspective are the experiences we seek in bringing our lives into the labyrinth. With God's help, we may be as startled as St. Paul or as relieved as occasionally being glad we are alive. Change of any kind, however, may be counted as success. Recollection doesn't result in all or none or sick or well, miserable or happy. We experience more or less, better or worse. We only do what we can to handle something better, to suffer less. To gain the most from walking the labyrinth and gain it more quickly, we must have the heart and will to keep going forward in our lives, in conversation with God.

# Assessing Your Grit

There isn't a more necessary modern skill than resiliency. We live with challenges that in the best circumstances require courage and risk tolerance. In more traumatic circumstances, we must come to terms with our feelings and behaviors even when we haven't yet absorbed them. Modern living is hard and complicated.

I'm thinking particularly of the information we get from political and social situations in war zones. A report or story about horrific events, such as school shootings or the slaying of zoo animals, calls forth thoughts and feelings that must be managed. Even the awareness that our technological heroism may be mistaken, such as the Jade Rabbit lunar rover dying on the moon, may cause us consternation and concern. Add to the situation the fact that some of this information isn't even personal, but we know about it in detail anyway. Things are simply just out of our control.

It may be hard to believe, at first, that regularly walking the labyrinth can help us manage our reactions to the sensations and perceptions that bombard us in our information-saturated environments. Believe me, it can, because walking the labyrinth builds resiliency.

Resiliency guides and protects us. It makes us feisty; it helps us have confidence in our abilities to lead self-sufficient lives full of puzzles we can attempt to solve, to use insight and spiritual strength to live stable and rewarding lives. Often it is our personal resiliency that encourages us and allows us to ask for support and help. This is especially true when we ask God, through prayer, for perseverance.

By walking the labyrinth, we may find in its spatial patterns and slowed time demands a successful response to the matters we wrestle with in our hectic and distracting lives.

# A Time to Be Mindful

When we are mindful, we feel rested and content, although we remain awake and alert. The sensations and perceptions we usually experience as a result of internal and external stimulation are slowed down. They are still bombarding us, but we are less attentive to them. Their urgency is diminished. We take our time, all the time we need, to accommodate them.

Being mindful is a more serene encounter with ourselves and the world around us. We have permission to drift a bit as we think and feel and act. This deliberate or mindful meditation isn't evasive. It is a choice we make to change channels. Instead of being pressed into motion, we ask ourselves to be quiet.

When we walk the labyrinth, we enter this special quiet space. The walk quiets our steps. We slow our pace. The walk suggests that we hear only the whispers of our hearts because we don't speak unless it's time for communal prayer or conversation. We observe unique and polite manners in order to leave quiet space for others. We actively breathe correctly in order to nourish our bodies and spirits.

Walking the labyrinth, alone or with others, awakens us into a state of mind that is much harder to experience (unless we practice) in everyday living. It's a special time and place because we suspend the usual and dare to suspect there is so much more to our experience. We allow for being our best selves. We strip away the worries, the demands, the motivations, and all the trappings of our lives in order to be mindful of what really is and might be. We quietly search while we walk, aware that there are answers of all sorts, all around. Perhaps an inkling will brush by; maybe an insight will shine forth. Looking forward, we are mindful.

# Blare and Glare

So much of modern life is exciting and stimulating, and that suits most of us part of the time. We are motivated to keep up with the demands of knowing as much as we can, performing at our best, and staying on top. If we are smart about it, get the right amount of sleep, make the best nutritional choices, and put some time into exercise, we are golden.

There is something lacking in this pretty picture. Don't read on unless you dare to consider there is probably very little respite in your routine and you need some. Respite is an important pause, a rest, time away to breathe and think and feel something besides the rush of living.

Living well requires that we sort through our daily choices. Like accomplishing our spiritual goals, such as making time for prayer, we have to arrange and plan for respite. It can't just happen, and you know it usually doesn't in the day-to-day hubbub. Our lives are spent in the blare and glare of the technology age. We are distracted by the sounds and lights urging us to keep going, rather than looking forward to our health and happiness.

Walking the labyrinth is a practice, really a tool that helps us dial back and shut out the blare and glare. In place of the demands and the distractions, the labyrinth focuses our attention on our inner lives. We come to experience our private thoughts and feelings. We exalt in our personal worth, detached for fifteen or twenty minutes or an hour from the external conditions of worth. Dare I suggest we find ourselves?

And the most interesting aspect of walking the labyrinth is that we can do it together, if we wish. Community doesn't invade our respite at all.

# Finding and Giving in the Labyrinth

"The meaning of life is to find your gift; the purpose of life is to give it away," said Picasso. I often think of his remark when I stand at the edge of the labyrinth before stepping into a walk. The labyrinthine design draws me to recall Picasso's paintings at certain periods of his work. Looking at these paintings has a similar effect on my thoughts and feelings as walking the labyrinth affords.

Finding our gifts is not easy. We have to reflect on our possibilities and potentials. We have to practice our choices. We have to grow into our excellence. Finding our gifts and their meanings is a task for us as individuals as well as a communal effort. No one finds his or her gift alone. The world in which we live helps to form our self-awareness and our self-appraisal. We succeed in a context, whether in spite of it or because of it.

Sometimes, as we go about living and working, our gifts come naturally to us, or so it seems. Sometimes something stops us in our tracks, and we have to take the time we need to consider our gifts. Walking the labyrinth provides an opportunity for discerning and envisioning our gifts. The experience of walking forward to the center and returning clarifies the direction of our lives, and meaning and purpose when we seek it.

Finding, however, is not keeping. That brings up the matter of giving our gifts away. Walking the pathway of the labyrinth, we may dare to consider if and how we are to share them. Gifts are not important when they are hoarded. Gifts are of no benefit if they are scattered. Our gifts have a purpose to serve when they are given in gratitude to others, whether in formal or informal ways. Walking the labyrinth provides encouragement for finding and giving.

# The Labyrinth and Time for Reflection

The quiet of the labyrinth beckons us to reflection. Standing at the start of a walk, we pause to discern what purpose we might have.

Reflection may include those things we need to let go of in order to find space within ourselves for the joy and jolliness of the season. Evelyn Underhill, mystic and author, suggests we pray.

> O Lord, penetrate those murky corners where we hide memories and tendencies on which we do not care to look, but which we will not disinter and yield freely up to you, that you may purify and transmute them. The persistent buried grudge, the half-acknowledged enmity, which is still smoldering; the bitterness of loss we have not turned into sacrifice, the private comfort we cling to, the secret fear of failure, which saps our initiative and is really inverted pride; the pessimism which is an insult to your joy - Lord, we bring all these to you, and we review them with shame and penitence in your steadfast light.

Reflection may lift us above the ordinary to find a truer inspiration for our life's journey. Reflection strengthens our resolve to express thanksgiving, gratitude, and love. We take this opportunity to take the time we need to feel and think our way into meaning and wisdom. Contentment, wrote Francis de Sales in the sixteenth century, is feeling the providential care of God. God's supreme gift feels as a child feels going out for a walk with his or her parents. Holding hands, picking fruit, and delighting in the world might be the path to cheer and joy for all of us.

These reflections and so many more come easily while walking the labyrinth.

# Just Breathe

"Breathing is the first act of life, and the last," remarked Joseph Pilates, describing the foundational principle of his fitness method. "Therefore, above all, learn how to breathe correctly."

Walking the labyrinth is the perfect place to learn and practice breathing. Stop at a place of your choice on your walk. Place your feet flat about a hip width apart on the pathway or in the center or along the boundary. Put one hand on each side of your lower rib cage with your fingertips touching. This gives you a tactile point of reference so your breathing is regular and rhythmical. Slowly breathe in through your nose. Visualize the movement of your diaphragm and feel your ribs move laterally into your waiting hands. Your fingertips will separate to accommodate your breath-expanded diaphragm. Don't lift your shoulders; let your mind and core muscles do the work.

Then reflect on exhaling. Your body's core is like a cylinder from the pelvic floor to the diaphragm. Breath fills the cylinder when you inhale and leaves the cylinder when you exhale. Rest your hands lightly on your rib cage. Exhale through pursed lips until your fingertips meet. Exhale as fully as you can.

Inhaling and exhaling in this way is called cleansing breath. It is a ritual that improves with practice and customization. It brings refreshment, calmness, and deep inner satisfaction. Outwardly, you sense a keenness of perception and a quickening of energy.

Breathing in silent concentration and reflection during your walk in the labyrinth lets you experience the path to a healthy center. You may find cleansing breath to be your habit in and out of the labyrinth.

# Labyrinth Meditation

The place to start a meditative walk in the labyrinth is before you step on the path. Prepare to be open to the unexpected places the walk will take you. Stand at the entrance for a period of time and think about yourself. What feelings or images, needs or concerns occur to you? Calmly gaze at the patterns that make the labyrinth. Commit to a self-contained experience, free from distractions. Walking the labyrinth is a gift to you. There is a treasure to be found and cherished.

As you walk inward toward the center of the labyrinth, breathe deeply and relax your body. Trust the path to guide you to a significant thought, feeling, image, or insight. These may come to you in simple ways or in flashes of the miraculous. You may notice things around you as though for the first time. Serenity may evolve from the peacefulness you discover. Resilience might shape your perspective of something troubling. You might identify a new source of energy to carry you forward. Pay attention to yourself as you walk.

Time spent at the center of the labyrinth allows you to deepen the meditative state of your mind and body. Here you can acknowledge that you are a seeker, a pilgrim, and a petitioner on a life's journey of your own. Here you can recognize the support you are ready to ask for or accept. Here you can frame the love that keeps you strong in the most personal way. Don't hurry out of this part of your walk. Take the time you need.

Walking outward on the spiraling path, you may now be somewhat lost in your sense of time and space. Have confidence in the pattern to make you feel safe. The pace may be slowed; your thoughts may be fleeting and disorganized. Try to give up routines of self-observation. Refrain from judging yourself. Take advantage of the remaining minutes of the walk for appreciating what you've gained from walking the labyrinth.

# Spiritual Transformation

# Walking the Labyrinth as a Spiritual Practice

The joy I feel when I walk the labyrinth transcends age. I was uplifted when I was young. I was energized when I was a busy professional in midlife. Now I am astounded by the appreciation I feel for this contemplative opportunity. I am a mature adult in the prime of my life, and I realize how much I value this particular spiritual practice.

There is purpose and meaning that reveals itself as I walk the labyrinth. I have an increased awareness of aging and its importance. Walking guides me in adapting to changes that accompany my sense that time is more and more precious. I have thoughts of cherishing myself as I am right now. I feel the letting go of who I was in favor of who I am. I look forward to the challenges, struggles, and surprises that make my life unique. I believe God is with me as I walk. I feel heartened on each and every walk.

Most of what I know about the purpose of living a long, active life I learned from boating with my grandfather and praying with my grandmother. They were the ideal people I loved best as a child. One from my mother, the other from my father, they are still my guides. They both prized healthy bodies, satisfying relationships, and most importantly, earnest spiritual lives. I always knew I couldn't go wrong if I followed their paths. The spiraling path of the labyrinth is more than a metaphor for me.

Walking the labyrinth raises my expectations not only of following my grandparents' example but also of developing my own spiritual goals. I know meditation is an essential part of mind, body, and spiritual wellness. I think I need thoughtful moments, freedom to imagine, and time to feel around inside my inner privacy. Truly, walking the labyrinth facilitates these experiences for me. I am grateful for it. My life is enriched because of my devotion to it.

## Strengthening Your Faith

When you enter the labyrinth, there is an immediate sense of flow. The path starts to spiral, and your steps change pace. You know this is a novel place. You feel ready to surrender to the design. You immediately give up any idea of making something happen here. You release your will to control the walk. In fact, you are aware that there is no longer the need to decide anything about the walk. An easy acceptance settles over you. Things will flow as they will, and you will flow with them.

How does this flow experience connect with faith? How is faith strengthened by "letting go and letting flow" do its work in the labyrinth?

Faith flows naturally out of love for your relationship with God. A sense of security and centeredness is present because God is always there in your thoughts and feelings. You're in a state of perpetual trust in God's sight. Vulnerabilities, imperfections, and life's painful experiences are balanced by the significance of your faith.

I'm suggesting that the experience in the labyrinth and the experience of faith are linked. Flow leads to learning and to exchange and to relating in both instances.

People thrive through a strong faith. They value and respect each other. They give and receive trust. They serve one another from a genuine love and concern.

Walk the labyrinth with other people sometimes. I guarantee your faith will be affected and strengthened.

# Labyrinth Walking and Creativity

Where do writers and painters find their inspiration? How are creative artists motivated to work? What's behind the impulse to create something novel and artful? Perhaps many of us ask ourselves these and other questions about our own creativity.

I want to suggest that walking the labyrinth assists in manifesting creativity, especially when walking routinely happens. Matthew Fox, an Episcopal priest, says that creativity is the time and place "where the divine meets the human." He suggests that "the most prayerful, most spiritually powerful act a person can undertake is to create, at his or her own level, with a consciousness of the place from which that gift arises." Walking the labyrinth has an ambiance that encourages us to focus our attention on our personal creative impulses. It quiets the mind to make space for transformation of vague notions into potentials and beyond into actions. As the walk goes forward, the spirit of creativity can soar.

As this spirit shines, sometimes in spite of ourselves, there develops a sense that if we keep on the path maybe it's possible to create something different from what we do in everyday living. Perhaps we contain within ourselves more and better talents than we acknowledge. We might perceive that being busy and productive isn't the only goal in life. A realization may waft over us that other "contents" need to be worked out of ourselves. With these experiences our mood changes. We may accept that the divine, likely, is breathing on us. What a fantastic idea that is! Anything is possible. "All is well, and all manner of things shall be well," said Julian of Norwich. We may become, quite literally, part of God's creation.

As we return along the labyrinth path, we may feel eager to share the gifts of insight the walk has facilitated. Yes, we respond, I will make beauty, I will give blessings, and I will bring my best self to my community. In thanksgiving for my creativity, I will grow my heart.

# Making the World Our Own

Walking the labyrinth with a point of reference, such as prayer, makes a sacred space for meditation and pious contemplation. The time intentionally set aside for praying creates a yearning for an opportunity to connect with the divine while traversing a human space. Encountering the magic and mystery of personal existence leads to joy, meaning, hope, and peace as we walk in and out of the labyrinth absorbed in prayer.

When the focus is prayer, walking the labyrinth is a significant statement of faith in God. The walking becomes a journey in Christian symbolism in anticipation of meeting God on the spiraling path of the labyrinth and of life. Walking acts as a meditative service equal to reciting the psalms and canticles and the reading of scripture. Meditation highlights the continuity in time between finite human experiences and the infinity of God.

It is not unusual to experience encouragement, gratitude for blessings, and even startling inspiration while walking the labyrinth. Frequently increased calm, clarifying insight, release, and rejuvenation and healing occur. Combining walking and praying yields both dark and light moments just as living does. Being perplexed is followed by joyfulness, confusion follows hope, and sometimes hurt and hope tumble over each other until there is simply curiosity at the power of God's spirit.

Walking the labyrinth in prayer is like planting a fairy garden with seeds collected from other spiritual events in life. As with any garden venture, at first the garden sleeps, then it creeps, and later, God willing, it leaps. That's precisely why some people walking the labyrinth start to dance, some get up on tiptoes, and some are apt to skip. The spirit moves everything: plants and flowers, wind and water, human minds and hearts. All that people have to do is walk and pray.

# Healing Meditation in the Labyrinth

Meditation is widely recognized as an adjunct to therapies and other healing strategies in health settings. There are examples of meditation that enhances relaxation in prolonged treatments. Praise abounds for the clarity of mind that meditation induces for understanding and bearing chronic illnesses. Meditative visualization allows healing to proceed more quickly and consistently because it encourages people to imagine a premeditated scenario of health. Meditation connects people to their intuition and mobilizes their spirituality to help meet health challenges.

Illnesses and their treatment often result in people feeling lost. They are cut off from the spiritual purposes of their lives and the meaningfulness of their life's journey. Opportunities to connect with God and to spiritual experiences become fewer and further removed from the events brought by illness and treatments. People may recognize the need for changing their mindset and their circumstances, but usual behaviors are no longer useful to accomplish those goals. It takes every bit of energy simply to cope with the problems. Another approach, such as walking or using the labyrinth, must be introduced.

Walking the labyrinth or using a finger labyrinth for meditation is remarkably effective in promoting healing. It frees people to focus in a unique and different way. It inspires new outlooks. Positive feelings and hopes spring from quiet reflection in the labyrinth. Expressing renewed commitment to personal wants and needs is easier during a contemplative time in the labyrinth. Trusting as a result of being in the labyrinth ignites self-worth and creates an enhanced perception of one's value in the world. The shortages of energy, money, or companionship inherent in dealing with ill health and the healing process suddenly seem less consequential with the help of meditative walks in the labyrinth.

More and more labyrinths are being built on hospital grounds and in mental health facilities. Healing gardens are appearing in communities all over the world. People are bringing life to the labyrinth. The labyrinth is a space that renews life, even rekindles the life of the spirit, with heartfelt use.

# Be Ready for Surprises as You Walk the Labyrinth

I was facilitating a group walk in an outdoor labyrinth on a cold but pleasant day. The people who ventured out in early spring on Cape Cod to spend thirty-five minutes slowly walking in brisk air surely had only one common intention. They wanted to walk the labyrinth for whatever surprises might be in store. They brought a playful mood to the experience. All of them felt exhilarated in the fresh air. Their eagerness shone on their smiling faces.

We began the walk with a brief focusing exercise. I suggested, "Thinking about God's enduring presence in our lives is always reassuring and often leads to serene feelings during a walk in the labyrinth. Today, however, let's think about the surprises we might experience as we walk. Let's notice the random thoughts or feelings that might come up." I talked about a research survey that found that one in eight people report hearing holy voices or seeing spiritual visions. "Whether entirely explainable or not, let's be ready for surprises as we walk the labyrinth."

There was laughter and some joking as we quieted ourselves before stepping into the labyrinth. The sounds of wind and the "early" bird songs replaced our voices as we set out on our journey in search of surprises. Each person appeared to adopt a sincere individual focus as though expecting to find a treasure just ahead.

At the end of the walk, we gathered for sharing. There was hilarity and fun in the words and actions of the group. The group wasn't any less connected as a result of our personal experiences in the walk. However, the enrichment and inspiration that came from the humor of the "surprises" we shared was uplifting for all of us. God is ready to surprise us - what an idea!

# Take a Strengthening Walk in the Labyrinth

There are times in life when stale routines, money problems, quarrels, and turned backs leave us depleted. We realize energy is low; we find ourselves at a dead end and in darkness. We feel bad; we feel living is asking too much of us. There is no compassion to be found, and we have lost our daring and persistence. We are in a sorry state!

Walking into the labyrinth provides some nourishment. Walking into the labyrinth promises some gladness and hope. Walking into the labyrinth offers encouragement to journey from bad to better.

As we release our bruised hearts and our harried minds to the fresh rhythms of the pathway, we open to music and laughter and celebration of life. As we reflect in the center of the labyrinth, the very air changes as our spirits are uplifted. On the return walk out of the labyrinth, we lose our confusion. We find the strength to go back into the strain and stress of living. We are renewed. Something marvelous has happened!

I believe God is present when we seek to pray and meditate by walking the labyrinth. The transformation of our human perspectives occurs because we enter the spiral of faith and retreat from the negative preoccupations of life. Embracing this sacred time and space for communicating with God is life enhancing. We rediscover our strengths, and we share with each other the common intention to ask for help. We become different as we recover from our indifference to God's grace. We have to do this more often!

# Engaging the Labyrinth

After much experience facilitating labyrinth walks, I have a mantra that guides my interactions with people: engagement is caught not taught! I can't teach it, only model it. I can't motivate it, only encourage it. People come to walk the labyrinth with some inclination or curiosity, but the level of engagement in the walk varies greatly.

With a reassuring, warm welcome, and equipped with my own eagerness and high level of engagement, I offer people the simple opportunity to know the walk. As is true of myself, no one knows everything about the experience. Through practice, however, what isn't known can slowly be understood and result in a deep, personal understanding. I urge people to recognize that what you don't know today, you might feel or know the next time. Engagement is a process. It demands attention, intention, and, above all, practice.

There are at least two aspects of engagement that are part of the labyrinth experience. Firstly, the individual determines his or her level of engagement during the walk and subsequent walks. The context in which engagement happens is a unique combination of interior and external events. Since the ritual is focused on walking, not talking, a person has the freedom to proceed according to what he or she desires. Just as the pace of the walk is personal, the speed and depth of engagement is idiosyncratic.

Secondly, engaging others on a walk may be included or excluded as useful and important parts of people's experience. Some walks may be more communal while at other times the sense of companionship may be more abstract. Enjoying a variety of different types of walks is probably the best advice I have for individuals and groups. Successful engagement in the practice of walking the labyrinth equals satisfaction either way.

Made in the USA
Charleston, SC
19 December 2014